ΛLETHEIΛ
ELEUTHEROO:
TRUTH WARRIORS OF THE SUPERNATURAL

ALETHEIA
ELEUTHEROO:
TRUTH WARRIORS OF THE SUPERNATURAL
Establishing the Glory of the Godhead

James Maloney, DD, ThD, PhD

WESTBOW
PRESS
A DIVISION OF THOMAS NELSON

WestBow Press books may be ordered through booksellers or by contacting:

WestBow Press
A Division of Thomas Nelson
1663 Liberty Drive
Bloomington, IN 47403
www.westbowpress.com
1-(866) 928-1240

Scripture taken from the New King James Version. Copyright 1979, 1980, 1982 by Thomas Nelson, inc. Used by permission. All rights reserved.

Scripture taken from the King James Version of the Bible.

ISBN: 978-1-4908-0045-5 (sc)
ISBN: 978-1-4908-0046-2 (hc)
ISBN: 978-1-4908-0044-8 (e)

Library of Congress Control Number: 2013912075

Printed in the United States of America.

WestBow Press rev. date: 8/8/2013

DEDICATION

To the late Dr. Chuck Flynn: for his fathering heart, always open to give me and others sound counsel; I greatly appreciated his propensity toward the Word—a deep theologian, yet one who always permitted the Spirit of God to move prophetically through him in honor of the supernatural. He was a man who bridged the generations, from the Latter Rain movement, into the charismatic renewal, and on into the prophetic restoration and beyond. He will be sincerely missed, and eagerly anticipated when I arrive in heaven.

And to Dr. Mary Ann Flynn: for her noble example as a woman of God, a theologian, a wonderful teacher and student of the Word, who was always supportive of her husband, honoring the Spirit, and possessed of a true mothering heart toward her family and her extended, spiritual family. My sincerest condolences and greatest honor to you, Mrs. Flynn.

⫘ Acknowledgments ⫘

I'd like to thank my family: my wife, Joy; my son, Andrew; and my daughter-in-law, Christy, for all their hard work and contributions. They invested hours of painstaking research and editing to help present this book to you. Thanks, guys!

καὶ γνώσεσθε τὴν ἀλήθειαν, καὶ ἡ ἀλήθεια ἐλευθερώσει ὑμᾶς.
—John 8:32

Aletheia eleutheroo (uh-LAY-they-uh eh-loo-they-RAH-oh)—
Greek (transliterated): "truth will free."

Aletheia (Strong's #225): "what is true in any matter under consideration, truly, in truth, according to truth, of a truth, in reality, in fact, certainly; what is true in things appertaining to God and the duties of man, moral and religious truth in the greatest latitude; the true notions of God which are open to human reason without His supernatural intervention; the truth as taught in the Christian religion, respecting God and the execution of His purposes through Christ, and respecting the duties of man, opposing alike to the superstitions of Gentiles and inventions of Jews, and the corrupt opinions and precepts of false teachers even among Christians; truth as a personal excellence, the candor of mind which is free from affection, pretence, simulation, falsehood, deceit."

☷ TABLE ☷
OF CONTENTS

☷ THE TRUTH OF ☷
SOUND DOCTRINE

So you are probably asking yourself, "What in the world does *aletheia eleutheroo* mean?" Not a phrase you come across every day, right? It's transliterated Greek, and in our wonderful English tongue it means, "Truth will free;" as in John 8:32, "And you shall know the truth, and the truth shall make you free." So next time you're in a coffee shop, try dropping some ancient Greek on your friends. I've found it works for me.

Well, my dear friends, once again I've decided to break out the old keyboard to share with you some of my thoughts on living life in the Lord. One of the compliments (there was more than one!) to my first book, *The Dancing Hand of God*, was how conversational it seemed, as if I were talking to the reader one-on-one. And so, following another ancient Greek proverb, "If it ain't broke, don't fix it none," I've decided to write this book just like I talk. I apologize upfront, 'cause I don't always talk proper. Uh, "properly."

I came to a shocking realization the other day while I was perusing the bookstore of a well-known Bible college: there was not one modern book on Christian doctrine in the whole place. Nada. Tons of books on releasing the supernatural, moving in the glory, prophecy and evangelism—all wonderful! And I was pleased to see *The Dancing Hand of God* and *Panoramic Seer* there, but nothing on basic Christian doctrine. I found that odd; after all, it *was* a Bible college. Shouldn't there be some books on foundations of the faith?

The Lord, I believe, spoke to me and said, "One of the things lacking in My body today is a firm foundation in My Word." And it got me thinking, more and more we're seeing some strange things being taught behind the pulpits; and not just teaching, but experiencing manifestations, strange phenomenon, that might be fleshly, but it could be demonic, too. I don't think most of these preachers are being malicious (although some probably are); it's just, with this new thrust into supernatural experiences that we're seeing in the charismatic church as a whole, and as the Lord is ramping up a greater expression of Himself in these "last days," (whatever that means) many ministers don't have the time to study properly the foundations of our Christian faith.

(This isn't a blanket statement covering the whole of the body— I trust you understand my intent. Many people *do* study.)

But because many of these well-meaning ministers, with powerful, miraculous expressions, are not rooted in a firm, un-shakeable foundation of Christian doctrine, some of them get a little, uh, wonky in their theology. They say some strange things behind the pulpit that cause confusion, or in worse situations, false doctrine that leads people astray.

Anybody who knows me knows I endeavor to be a student of God's Word, to be resolutely entrenched in the black-and-white letter of the Bible. My previous books, I hope, went to great lengths to establish that I believe in the vast majority of the teachings of the Word of Faith movement (note, I said *vast*, not *all*.)

But this isn't being taught as it should in most churches and Bible schools, so we have a multitude of people who are desperate for a touch of the supernatural power of God; but their fundamentals of faith are lacking, and it inhibits the flow of power. God does *nothing* apart from His Word. He places His Word above His name! (Psalm 138:2) His Spirit does *nothing* that is not backed up by the complete revelation of the written Word of God.

As Jesus said, "...You are mistaken, not knowing the Scriptures nor the power of God." (Matthew 22:29) There are two facets to being released in the supernatural: a firm understanding of what God's Word reveals about Himself, and a solid expression of God's power experienced through His Spirit. The Word and the Spirit, operating side-by-side, together.

Look, I'm a revivalist. I love the supernatural; I love the glory of God manifest in our lives. I've written books on it, and I want to write many, many more! But it takes an understanding of who He is, a true knowledge built on the truth of His Word, that creates those kinds of miracle-working warriors we all want to become.

It is the truth you know that will make you free. That means you have to *know* it!

PILGRIMS OF TRUTH

Our knowledge of truth is to be a progression. Peter's epistles admonish us as believers to be established and live in *present truth*. Truth is that which is absolutely and forever settled in God; it is this finality that is the springboard for our position in Him—truth cannot change and demands that *we* change around it.

The Holy Spirit of truth anoints us so that we can walk in obedience to the truth He reveals. Without the Spirit in manifestation, that anointing upon us, which is demonstration of the truth, we are left with simply "head knowledge." And while knowledge in general is good, it does not necessarily mean *truth*.

Since the Holy Spirit answers to the Word, it's important we have a basic understanding of what the Word says in order to exhibit the flow of anointing. We are required to be obedient to that truth we know, through the grace of the Spirit, which will free us to *experience* supernatural activity. In time, as we progress in truth, our experience catches up to our knowledge; they begin to move in tandem. And our experience/knowledge, then, coincides with our position in growing in the Lord; we are changed from glory to glory. (2 Corinthians 3:18)

We are "pilgrims... elect according to the foreknowledge of God the Father, in sanctification of the Spirit, for obedience and sprinkling of the blood of Jesus Christ..." (1 Peter 1:1-2) For what purpose are we sprinkled? "...receiving the end of your faith—the salvation of your souls." (1 Peter 1:9)

So if Peter says we are *receiving* (present tense), there is a process implying we have yet more to receive. See the progression?

Chosen pilgrims, according to the Father's plan, to be sanctified by the ministry of the Spirit, so we can be obedient to Jesus Christ, thus sprinkled with His precious blood.

(You have to say "pilgrim" with a John Wayne accent, by the way. That's one of the rules...)

Yes, our spirits were made new when we were born again, but there is change in our minds and souls as we grow in the Lord. That's why we need a strong foundation in truth. So, yes, we *are* saved, but we are *being* saved according to a progression in truth, and we *will be* saved at the coming of Jesus Christ.

> "Now may the God of peace Himself sanctify you completely; and may your whole spirit, soul, and body be preserved blameless at the coming of our Lord Jesus Christ. He who calls you is faithful, who also will do it..." and "...who delivered us from so great a death, and does [shall] deliver us; in whom we trust that He will still deliver us..."
> (1 Thessalonians 5:23-24; 2 Corinthians 1:10)

So in an effort to be obedient to what I believe the Lord directed me to do, I've written this to help, in some small way, compile some of the basic, fundamental truths of our faith all in one convenient handy-dandy, easy-to-read guidebook. It's not the end-all, be-all on doctrine—I wouldn't presume to be so arrogant—but it's a good place to start.

And I believe it will help release the glory and supernatural in a greater way in your life. Perhaps you're a stay-at-home mother, and you're a prophetess in your church. You have a gift, but you don't have the time to go to Bible school for two years. This book is for you. Perhaps the Lord's given you a healing anointing, and

5

it's burning your hands to be released on a hurting world that needs the Father's divine touch. But you feel pressed to get out there in the streets—now! This will help keep you balanced. You have the desire and the power, but you have to be willing to discipline yourself in an ever-increasing depth of knowledge of what God has said in His Word.

The very process of progressing in truth depends on your willingness to stretch, that is, to "add to" what you know already.

> "But also for this very reason, giving all diligence, add to your faith virtue, to virtue knowledge, to knowledge self-control, to self-control perseverance, to perseverance godliness, to godliness brotherly kindness, and to brotherly kindness love. For if these things are yours and abound, you will be neither barren nor unfruitful in the knowledge of our Lord Jesus Christ."
>
> (2 Peter 1:5-8)

You have faith, you know what you know, and you believe the Word of God is truth. Now add virtue (that's not just goodness or godly determination, but *expression* of virtue, a supernatural unction) to your faith. And knowledge (interpretation of Scripture.) Faith added to virtue added to knowledge will bring the above expressions (temperance and patience, holy living and—the greatest "stretching" of all: brotherly kindness) to those around you, culminating in the greatest expression: divine love. The display of the supernatural is rooted in divine love.

Remember this is to be a process of *adding*. Each "level" builds on the next; you can't omit what you added previously, or focus on one truth over the others (that leads to wild tangents.)

See why the progression in truth is so important? It releases the glory of God and the fruit of godly living.

This book is going to be a little different than my other books. *Aletheia Eleutheroo* is more of a doctrinal study guide, a textbook (hopefully not a boring one.) As such, it won't have all the wonderful testimonies and cool stories. But it will teach the Word of God, as best as I can; and it will be entertaining, hopefully. The concepts in this book are not "new" by any means, but perhaps I can, by God's grace, provide a different perspective on why a firm foundation in Christian doctrine is so vitally essential to releasing the supernatural. The whole thrust of this book is to inground (I totally made that word up) you in the truth so that the miraculous, the glory, the supernatural is released in your life in a deeper way. It's basic, but it's necessary. Simple, and profoundly important. It's not hard to understand, but you'd have to read dozens of old-time books, whereas I've compiled a lot of truths here in our modern speech.

You're welcome.

This does not replace the need to read your Bible, to go to school or seminary (as the Lord directs you) and to study to show yourself approved.

"Be diligent to present yourself approved to God, a worker who does not need to be ashamed, rightly dividing the **word of truth**." (2 Timothy 2:15, emphasis added)

This book is to be added into your daily time learning about the Lord. I've just tried to make it a little easier, that's all. The truth is out there (that's probably copyrighted), and it *will* make you free. So here we go...

⚏ THE TRUTH OF ⚏
THE BIBLE

The truth starts with the Bible. Without the Bible, we are incapable of understanding and implementing the truth to make us free. The expressions of the supernatural attributes of God are rooted in His Word. So the Bible is a good place to begin, right?

The written (Greek, *graphe*, Strong's #1124, "grof-EH") Word of God that you have, in whichever translation you prefer, is the Greek word *logos*. (Strong's #3056, "LAH-goss") Referring to the Bible, *logos* is speech used with a living voice, words, a discourse, explanation, reason, judgment, doctrine, commandment, order, mandate, decree, a divine plan, and the revelation of God's mind on a particular subject (the salvation of mankind.)

It implies a complete thought, the totality of what needs to be said, from start to finish. *Logos* reveals the speaker's complete concept: in the case of the Bible, the plan of salvation culminating in the death, resurrection and ascension of Jesus Christ. It fully provides the thoughts and plans of God the Father on bridging the gap between mankind and deity, how to do it, how to maintain it, how to share it with others. The Bible is the guidebook, the instruction manual, and it is complete and total in its scope for sharing the historical, chronological and spiritual means by which man can approach God.

Logos is different from *rhema* (another Greek word for "word," Strong's #4487, kinda said like "HRAY-mah.") *Rhema* can mean a singular word of thought, something taken out of the entire *logos*. An idea that is voiced by Someone (in this case, the Holy Spirit.) It means "to pour forth." The implication is that when a Christian reads the *logos* of God, His Spirit will pull a portion or a thought of it out (*rhema*) to the reader for deeper understanding of the concept. So, prophetic words inspired by the Spirit are *rhemas* of God's *logos* revealed in the *graphe* Word of God, which is why *rhema* is always subject to the entirety of *logos*. *Logos* is the Bible, *rhemas* are passages of the *logos*.

> "In Him you also trusted, after you heard the **word of truth**, the gospel of your salvation; in whom also, having believed, you were sealed with the Holy Spirit of promise..."
>
> (Ephesians 1:13, emphasis added)

The word of truth is the *logos* of *aletheia*—thus, the revelation of what is in the Bible makes you free, and once we believe in Him who gave that word of truth, we are given the promise of the Holy Spirit, the Instigator of grace-works in our lives (i.e., supernatural expression) and the Developer of godly character and living (i.e., fruit of the Spirit.)

Ah, but you may be saying, "How do I *know* that the Bible I have is God's true *logos*? What about the different translations, or errors in translation? Isn't it just written by a bunch of old men from thousands of years ago?"

(Why is it we think of the writers of the Bible as always old guys with white beards and robes? Or maybe I'm the only one...)

THE INSPIRATION OF LOGOS

Paul tells his spiritual son, Timothy, that:

> "All Scripture is given by inspiration of God, and is profitable for doctrine, for reproof, for correction, for instruction in righteousness, that the man of God may be complete, thoroughly equipped for every good work."
>
> (2 Timothy 3:16-17)

"Inspiration" is *theopneustos* (Strong's #2315, "they-OP-noose-toss"), literally "God-breathed." Where are some other instances of God breathing?

"And the Lord God formed man of the dust of the ground, and breathed into his nostrils the breath of life; and man became a living being." (Genesis 2:7)

"And when He [Jesus] had said this, He breathed on them, and said to them, 'Receive the Holy Spirit.'" (John 20:22)

Yes, the Bible was written by a bunch of "old men." But under the inspiration (breathing) of God's Spirit. This is one of the key, unshakeable truths of the Christian foundation, and as such is the launching pad for every other truth regarding what we hold true as Christians: this belief that the Bible is *inerrant and infallible*, inspired by God through man, to man. Without an unwavering belief in this truth, everything contained in the Bible is left open to one's own private interpretation of any given part. So a person could say, Hey, I believe this part of the Bible about not killing people and not stealing, but this part about Jesus Christ being God in the flesh, nah, I don't buy that.

It's an all-or-nothing principle; one cannot pick and choose. The *logos* is above contestation. It is an act of *faith* on the behalf of the believer, as the author of Hebrews points out:

"For indeed the gospel was preached to us as well as to them; but the word which they heard did not profit them, not being mixed with faith in those who heard it." (Hebrews 4:2)

> "And so we have the prophetic word confirmed [we also have the more sure prophetic word], which you do well to heed as a light that shines in a dark place, until the day dawns and the morning star rises in your hearts; knowing this first, that no prophecy of Scripture is of any private interpretation [origin], for prophecy never came by the will of man, but holy men of God spoke [but men spoke from God] as they were moved by the Holy Spirit."
> (2 Peter 1:19-22)

The words in brackets are from the marginal notes of the New King James—I didn't make them up myself. So, Peter's saying the Bible is not originated in the will of man, but men spoke as God directed them by His Spirit.

Thus, the Bible is not just words from "old men," so much as "old men" relating what they heard from God's Spirit. If we believe this to be truth, in faith, then the Bible was made the way it is by God's own hand through mankind.

(I'm using the term "old men" humorously, hence my clever use of quotation marks.)

God can communicate to believers through *revelation*, the truth from God's heart directly into the person's heart. Reveal means "uncover." The Spirit uncovers the thoughts of God and reveals them to man. Paul, in Galatians 1:11-12, shows that his doctrine came directly through the Lord Jesus Christ, not from earthly teaching.

> "But as it is written: 'Eye has not seen, nor ear heard, nor have entered into the heart of man the things which God has prepared for those who love Him.' But God has revealed them to us through His Spirit. For the Spirit searches all things, yes, the deep things of God. For what man knows the things of a man except the spirit of the man which is in him? Even so no one knows the things of God except the Spirit of God. Now we have received, not the spirit of the world, but the Spirit who is from God, that we might know the things that have been freely given to us by God."
>
> (1 Corinthians 2:9-12)

God revealed Himself to the writers of the Bible and inspired them to write the thoughts of God down after they were revealed by the Spirit. The very words themselves are inspired of God, breathed on by the Spirit.

It is not that the Spirit overcomes and possesses the writer, physically moving his hand like some automaton, or dictating verbatim what was to be written, or that they were caught up in a trance-like state (although much revelation did come from visions and dreams); but the thoughts that the writer communicates to paper are implanted there under the Spirit's guidance, using his own references based on cultural/historical perspective and personality. Therefore the Bible was written by God through man.

In His infinite wisdom, He chose to utilize the abilities of man (which are given by God anyway) to say what He wanted to say to humanity. The point is, it is through His wisdom that man wrote.

"These things we also speak, not in words which man's wisdom teaches but which the Holy Spirit teaches, comparing spiritual things with spiritual." (1 Corinthians 2:13)

To drive this point home, let's look again at 2 Peter 1:21, that part "moved" by the Holy Spirit. That's the Greek word *phero*. (Strong's #5342, "FAIR-oh" with the R trilling: "*rrr*") It means "driven as a ship with forceful speed," like in Acts 27:15: the ship that Paul was on was "driven" (*phero*); it's also the same word used in Acts 2:2 for "rushing" (*phero*) mighty wind.

God is alive, and as He cannot be separated from His Word, therefore, His Word is alive. It breathes as He breathes.

> "For the word of God is living and powerful, and sharper than any two-edged sword, piercing even to the division of soul and spirit, and of joints and marrow, and is a discerner of the thoughts and intents of the heart."
>
> (Hebrews 4:12)

"...Through the word of God which lives and abides forever." (1 Peter 1:23) "...The words that I speak to you are spirit, and they are life." (John 6:63)

Okay, I know this is tons of scripture, but since we are studying the Word, it necessitates a lot of quotes. At least, I've saved you the time of tracking all these down, right?

So, what are we saying here? God breathed *Himself* into the words that make up the Bible in your hands, so in turn, the *logos* of God is a living substance. He *is* His Word. His Word is God—They are one and the same. His Word is eternal and sure.

Now, let's take this a step further—and I bet you see where I'm going with this. Jesus Christ *is* the *Logos* of God. He is the Word made flesh. He is the sum total of the thoughts of God concerning mankind, the entirety of this creation of which we are a part.

> "In the beginning was the Word, and the Word was with God, and the Word was God. He was in the beginning with God. All things were made through Him, and without Him nothing was made that was made. In Him was life, and the life was the light of men... And the Word became flesh and dwelt among us, and we beheld His glory, the glory as of the only begotten of the Father, full of grace and truth."
>
> (John 1:1-4,14)

"...And His name is called The Word of God." (Revelation 19:13)

The Spirit illuminates the truth of the Word to believers. This can be *rhemas* of the *logos*. It isn't through human reason, because we cannot fully understand the Bible with our own logic. We are strongly warned in Revelation 22 not to add to the Word; our natural reasoning is faulty.

> "But the natural man does not receive the things of the Spirit of God, for they are foolishness to him; nor can he know them, because they are spiritually discerned. But he who is spiritual judges all things, yet he himself is rightly judged by no one. For 'who has known the mind of the Lord that he may instruct Him?' But we have the mind of Christ."
>
> (1 Corinthians 2:14-16)

As believers, we have the mind of Christ, discerning the truth in God's Word by His Spirit. Simple enough. I am not here to convince disbelievers, as I am writing to an audience who already is being saved by this knowledge. "For the message of the cross is foolishness to those who are perishing, but to us who are being saved it is the power of God." (1 Corinthians 1:18) So if we believe the Word is inspired, it is of necessity infallible, since an attribute of God is to be flawless.

THE INFALLIBILITY OF LOGOS

No other book in human history has undergone as much scrutiny and scholarly investigation as the Bible. People, believers and non-believers alike, have asked questions like, Is the Bible historically accurate? How reliable are the translations through the years? Are there errors in the print? Why are these books selected, and not these books? Which modern English translation is best? So on and so on. These kinds of questions are not without merit, but of course, no matter what kind of historical, internal or external evidence exists, one must choose by faith to believe the Bible is not only inspired by God, but is ultimately infallible as God is infallible (meaning "incapable of making a mistake.") But for the sake of diligence, let's quickly address some of these questions.

The Bible you hold in your hand as a Protestant Christian contains sixty-six books, split into an Old Testament of thirty-nine books, and a New Testament of twenty-seven books. It was written by some forty different authors over a sixteen hundred year period in three different languages. The authors were as varied culturally as they were geographically, from kings to tentmakers, across several countries. The fact that the Bible is completely unified without internal contradiction with all of the above variables is one of the greatest "proofs" in the validity of what the Bible says. It couldn't possibly have been masterminded by people alone.

The question of which English translation is best is most often left up to personal preference. For me personally, after studying each translation, I find the King James Version to be the best, even though there are minor translation errors now and again. (Note: the error is in the *translation*, not the original text.)

But whether the NIV, the NAS, the NKJ, the Amplified, the ESB—as it relates to God's revelation of the plan of salvation for mankind, each is nearly as good as the next.

It's not prudent as a Christian brotherhood to be divisive because such-and-such translation omits certain phrases (although certain translations walk a thin line, omitting certain key referrals to the blood of Christ in an effort to present the Bible as "less bloody"); or another translation uses "dragons" when it should be translated "jackals." This doesn't mean that we should accept just *any* translation as "authorized," but rather that as the Holy Spirit is the One who illuminates the scriptures to us, we by faith accept the infallibility of God's Word, even when *minor* grammatical or translation errors occur, provided the entirety of God's *logos* is unadulterated concerning Christian doctrine: the centrality of the Bible's message, Jesus Christ as Lord and Savior for the whole world.

We live in a digital age, where we have numerous translations readily at hand. Bible software, Bible websites, commentaries and concordances—all of these can be accessed from our *phones*, in most cases, nowadays. So, my suggestion to you is to study several translations, compare verses back and forth. You don't need a pile of cash to purchase a hundred leather-bound Bibles like you used to thirty years ago.

The books of the Bible were canonized (comes from a word meaning "measuring rod" incidentally) by withstanding certain tests, briefly highlighted below, and are recognized by the supreme vast majority of Christianity as being inspired by God.

Tradition holds that the Old Testament was compiled by the prophet Ezra, and the New Testament was approved in its form by the Fourth Century AD. The difference between a Catholic Bible and a Protestant Bible arises from the Apocrypha, fourteen books of the Old Testament added by the Roman Catholic Church. We as Protestants reject these books as canonized on the basis that they were never part of the original Hebrew scriptures (the Catholic Church added them in 1546, if memory serves); they were never mentioned in the New Testament by the Lord or the first-century apostles; and they were written in the historical timeframe between the Old and New Testaments (the prophet Malachi and the prophet John the Baptist) when there were no accepted prophecies by the Jews, on top of certain doctrines taught in them that are contrary to the rest of the canonized Word. Concepts such as suicide, Jesus perhaps having a love interest on earth, etc.

That is not to say there is nothing of merit in the books that do not appear in the canonical Protestant Bible, yet there is enough in the Word of God that makes the Apocrypha virtually unessential and superfluous. They are *not* inspired, and must always be viewed from that light, should you choose to read them.

And we must always remember, *everything* in *any* Christian book you read (that includes this one) is overruled by the Holy Bible when discrepancy appears. The Bible is the authoritative, bottom-line concerning the Father and His decrees for mankind. Period. Nothing needs to be added, nothing needs to be taken away. It is perfect.

(Also, as an aside, while technically Latter Day Saints do *not* call *The Book of Mormon, Another Testament of Jesus Christ* a "Bible," they do treat it as inspired scripture—the fifteen books of which mainstream Protestant Christianity rejects for the same reasons as the Apocrypha.)

So again, if we accept that the Bible is inspired and infallible in its original forms, we accept that God intended for us as English-speaking people to read the Bible we have in our hands.

This does not exclude the noble works of modern translators who, with deference to the original Greek and Hebrew scrolls, attempt to provide the most conclusive translations to the body of Christ, but again, it is an element of faith.

The Bible has been tested against accepted history, including other historical documents of the same age, and has been found meticulously accurate. The copies of the original manuscripts have completely passed rigorous historical testing; scholars from all walks of life attest to the principal accuracy of the translations from Hebrew and Greek.

There are something like 8,000 manuscripts of the Latin Vulgate alone, and a whole bunch of other statistics this old mind has forgotten, not to mention the, what, 350 Dead Sea Scrolls. There are nearly 200 translations of the Old Testament all entirely consistent in the most minute details historically across more than a thousand years—that feat in and of itself speaks of a supernatural element. I forget the mathematical chance of such an occurrence happening, but it was like 750 with twenty zeros after it or something like that.

The point is, the Bible is historically accurate, internally and externally. It has withstood every archeological discovery, and in fact, is supported by such finds. Lastly, and most importantly, there are over three hundred prophecies relating to the Messiah in the Old Testament that were fulfilled by Jesus Christ in the New Testament. The *Logos* Himself attests to the accuracy of the *logos* of God.

"Do not think that I came to destroy the Law or the Prophets. I did not come to destroy but to fulfill." (Matthew 5:17)

"As for God, His way is perfect; the word of the Lord is proven; He is a shield to all who trust in Him." (Psalm 18:30)

So since this book (the one you're reading right now, I mean) is a book about the supernatural, how does all this knowledge apply to you? Easy. The entirety of supernatural unction is rooted in, tied to and subjected under the *logos* of God. His Word is the foundation for every Christian not only to enter into any supernatural experience with the Lord, but it is to be the final judge of any such experience.

That's pretty important, if you pay attention to what was just said. The bottom line, for every Christian out there, the basis of how you *know* the truth that sets you free in a supernatural way is directly established in your knowledge of God's counsel as revealed in His Word. The Bible does not *explain away* a lack of supernatural activity; to the contrary, it shows what is needed in one's life for the anointing of God to be operating.

Thus, if the anointing is *not* flowing, the Bible will tell us why, as it is breathed upon by His Spirit. The Spirit permits Himself to be subject to the Word, and the Spirit displays the Word in action, always pointing to the kingship of the Lord Jesus Christ.

Enough said.

⛩ THE TRUTH OF ⛩ HERMENEUTICS

We have just highlighted the importance of the inspiration and infallibility of the Word of God. So what's next? It stands to reason that if we take the Word of God to be *THE* Word of God, shouldn't we study what it says? What is the point of inspiration if there is no interpretation: understanding what God meant by what He said. Let's take a few pages here and talk about hermeneutics, and how it can relate to a supernatural unction in our lives and ministries.

Hermeneutics. That's another funny old word that means "the interpretation and study of God's Word." Well, actually, the original word didn't apply to the Bible. It referred to Hermes, the Greek god of speech and writing. He was the gods' interpreter, which is why the Lycaonians thought Paul was Mercury (the Roman name for Hermes—I think in the NKJ they actually translate it Hermes, but I've got an old KJV open right now), since he was the chief speaker. (Acts 14:12)

For us, since we know Hermes is rubbish (sorry, ancient Greeks, it's true), we mean it as the science of interpreting the Bible, how to study God's Word correctly and systematically. It quite literally means, "untying (as in knots), solving a problem, expounding an idea thoroughly."

There are several types of sciences (I mean that as "systematic studies") that coexist with hermeneutics, and it is the application of all that presents the Christian with the most solid foundation in the Word of God.

So, when the God-approved translation of the Bible came to us, the science of determining which books of the Bible were truly inspired and which were not is called *canonology*. Other sciences are *historical criticism* (studying the authors themselves, the dates they lived in, how accurate are the historical references in the book, etc.); and *textual criticism* (testing the actual text itself, as far back as we have copies of the original manuscripts, for accurate translation.)

Bet you didn't realize Christians took this much time and energy to make sure the Bible is authoritative, huh? Yes, for centuries scholars have dedicated their lives to test the Bible for inerrancy, integrity and infallibility; of course, God orchestrating this through the ages to bring His untainted *logos* throughout history.

So we take hermeneutics (in our context, the interpretation of God's Word) along with the above sciences, and this forms our biblical theology as Christians. Alongside hermeneutics is *exegesis*, which comes from another really old Greek word, *ex-egeomai* (Strong's #1834, akin to "ex-uh-GAY-oh-my"), and it means, "to lead out."

When we talk about exegesis, it is the *execution of herme-neutics*. That means applying the principles of hermeneutics and putting them into action in interpreting the Word of God. Hermeneutics is the art; exegesis is the means. Hermeneutics deals with the entire umbrella of general interpretation, be that in speech or nonverbal communication or writing. Exegesis primarily deals with interpreting a written text and often a singular excerpt of text (like an individual scripture or passage.)

One who performs exegesis is an exegete. So next time you're at a Bible study, call your friends exegetes, and see if they think you're calling them names.

ALLOW ME TO EXEMPLIFY

Shall I share with you a fairly competent exegesis on 2 Thessalonians 1:3-5 as an example? Don't mind if I do! You can thank me later.

> "We are bound to thank God always for you, brethren, as it is meet, because that your faith groweth exceedingly, and the charity of every one of you all toward each other aboundeth; so that we ourselves glory in you in the churches of God for your patience and faith in all your persecutions and tribulations that ye endure: which is a manifest token of the righteous judgment of God, that ye may be counted worthy of the kingdom of God, for which ye also suffer..."
>
> (2 Thessalonians 1:3-5 KJV)

Now, let's draw the meaning out of this passage. Second Thessalonians was written about AD 55 while Paul was in Corinth, so that he could instruct the church at Thessalonica on the Day of the Lord and certain events immediately preceding that Day. He wanted to teach them about an apostasy (a falling away of the saints) that would happen, through seduction by Antichrist (a philosophy, doctrine, spirit, or even a person which says Christ and His anointing is capable of changing.)

False teachers had forged Paul's name to a letter claiming he had changed his doctrine, so Paul is here to assure them he had, indeed, *not* changed his doctrine. Go get 'em, Paul!

You'll see in a bit, one of the ways to study the Word of God is to personalize a passage of scripture for yourself, so in this instance, the ye's and your's mean "you." Yes, you, the reader—the one holding this book.

These verses talk about "glorying" (Greek, *kauchaomai*, Strong's #2744, "to boast or glory in a thing," kinda like "cow-HOW-my") in three facets of commendation:

1. Your faith grows exceedingly

Faith is the Greek word *pistis* (Strong's #4102, just like it looks: "PIS-tis") and means, "the conviction of the truth of anything, belief; in the NT of a conviction or belief respecting man's relationship to God and divine things, generally with the included idea of trust and holy fervor born of faith and joined with it; the conviction that God exists and is the creator and ruler of all things, the provider and bestower of eternal salvation through Christ; a strong and welcome conviction or belief that Jesus is the Messiah, through whom we obtain eternal salvation in the kingdom of God; the religious beliefs of Christians; belief with the predominate idea of trust (or confidence) whether in God or in Christ, springing from faith in the same; fidelity, faithfulness; the character of one who can be relied on."

Grows exceedingly is conveyed in the Greek word *hyperauxano* (Strong's #5232, "hooper-ex-ON-oh"), meaning, appropriately enough, "to increase beyond measure, to grow exceedingly."

2. Your love is abounding

The KJV translates "love" as "charity;" the NKJ has it as "love." **Love** is found in the Greek word *agape* (Strong's #26, "uh-GAH-pay") and means, "brotherly love, affection, good-will, love, benevolence." *Agape* goes beyond *phileo* (Strong's #5368, "fill-EH-oh," where "eh" is like egg, not hay) which speaks of friendly love, or to "like" someone a lot.

Abounding is the Greek word *pleonazo* (Strong's #4121, something like "play-oh-NOD-zoh"), meaning, "to superabound, to exist in abundance, to increase, be augmented, to make to increase."

3. Your patience and faith in all your persecutions and tribulations

Patience is *hypomone* (Strong's #5281, similar to "hoop-oh-moe-NAY"), meaning, "steadfastness, constancy, endurance, in the NT the characteristic of a man who is not swerved from his deliberate purpose and his loyalty to faith and piety by even the greatest trials and sufferings; patiently and steadfastly waiting for; patient enduring, sustaining, perseverance."

Persecutions is "persecutions." (Strong's #1375, *diogmos*, a bit like "deo-gwuh-MOSS") Deep, huh? But **tribulations** is the Greek *thlipsis* (Strong's #2347, "THLIP-sis"), and it means, "a pressing, pressing together, pressure; metaphorically, oppression, affliction, tribulation, distress, straits."

That's a lot of info, huh, from just three verses! What this has shown us is three-fold praise for the Thessalonians due to their growing faith, abounding love and patience in tribulation. Applying this to ourselves, there is glory to be found in a conviction of truth that grows beyond all measure, benevolent love toward others that superabounds in abundance, and steadfast endurance when we are pressed together in oppressive affliction and persecution. Hey, that'll preach!

SOME TECHNICAL STUFF

As exegetes in hermeneutics (see how that sounds cool?), there are certain philosophies Christians implement when studying the Word of God, some of which are better than others. Let's outline a few of these, because unless you're a theologian, you've probably not had much experience with these methodologies, although you may have been practicing them when reading the Bible and not knowing they had a name.

The best way to study the Word of God is *literally*. This is called the Literal Method, appropriately enough. What this means is the plain words written on the page in black and white mean what they say, and God meant them that way, therefore they are wholly reliable. Sometimes this is called the Grammatico-Historical Method, but that's too hard to say, so we call it "Literal." Now, keep in mind "literal" explains the primary intent of the author in light of the normal usage of his language, in his customary, cultural, historical context.

The proverbial Golden Rule of Hermeneutics is as follows: **"If the Plain Sense Makes Common Sense, Seek No Other Sense."** Memorize this, there's a test later.

Being a literalist to the Word of God doesn't mean you cannot perceive the words' spiritual applications. As a literalist you take the words to mean what they say, but you also recognize the Bible as a spiritual book talking about spiritual matters that can only be perceived, or truly understood, in your spirit (boy, that's repetitive!)

As literalists, we accept that the only way to interpret accurately the literal words is through the spiritual illumination of the Holy Spirit. That's pretty deep—take a second to meditate on that sentence.

This, also, does *not* exclude the fact that the author can write figuratively and it still be literal, because we are taking it in context. You and I speak figuratively all the time, but that doesn't make our communication any less literal. Does this make sense? Just because I say, "Boy, it's like a sauna out there today," doesn't mean I actually think it's like a real sauna—I'm speaking figuratively—but that doesn't negate the literal fact it is hot outside. Incidentally, it *is* hot outside today.

Lastly, before we outline the less adequate philosophies of hermeneutical studies, let's point out that taking the Word of God literally, in the context above, does not eliminate an application of what we've interpreted (in fact, it enhances it!) There can be dozens of practical applications of one portion of scripture that is accurately interpreted, see?

Also, being a literalist does not exclude that there are hidden levels of meaning to a particular exegesis—there can be (but not always) a deeper meaning to what is obviously stated. However, whatever buried meanings that are dug out of the literal black and white should always be set within the boundaries of what is frankly uncovered in the entirety of the Word.

Otherwise, you get factions in the body of Christ built upon one or two "odd" meanings to what is otherwise a fairly obvious implication that God laid out for His people to read. For example, snake-handlers. (Mark 16:18) The vast majority of us don't go kicking over rocks looking for rattlesnakes, and we're wise not to do so; but that doesn't negate the literal interpretation, as shown by Paul. (Acts 28:5)

Oh, here's an interesting aside on Acts 28:5 that wasn't included in the price of this book, but shows some more hermeneutical exegesis in action (and besides, it's kind of funny): in *Vincent's Word Studies*, on Luke's use, as a physician, of the word *therion* (Strong's #2342, "they-uh-REE-on" but the "th" is hard like thunder, not soft like they) as "beast" (in the KJV; also translated viper, serpent, reptile and creature in other translations), we find the Latin translation as *theriaca*, relating to the medical term of "antidote"—made primarily from the flesh of vipers—wherein we get the corrupted English word "treacle," or in our modern American speech "molasses." So molasses originally meant snake flesh. Yummy! Think of that next time you want a gingersnap.

Okay, that was free. Moving right along, let's quickly talk about some less beneficial methods of studying the Bible—just so you're aware of them, if you ever find yourself talking to someone who practices them.

The Rational Method is simply a way of describing the Bible in terms of disbelief. Irrationally (see, I punned), this method purports the Bible to be a human-made document, and natural, human reason is to be the conductor of interpreting an otherwise mythical old rag. True students of the Bible, who believe it to be inspired, should utterly reject this methodology. This is not to say we turn our rational minds off when we study the *logos* of God, but we filter our rationality through our spirits, and not the other way round.

The Allegory Method states that the Bible's plain meaning is not its real meaning, and that the true meaning is hidden beneath, and so one has to break apart the literal words to find that secret meaning underneath the obvious meaning. Meaning (another pun, I'm sorry) one simply has to believe that God did not say what He really meant. This adds a mystical quality to what is otherwise blatant. In fact, the Allegory Method is often called Mystical Method. Again, this leaves the student open to great potential error, since it's my experience God's usually pretty blunt and straightforward.

If one assumes scripture can have any number of meanings beyond the declarative text, it can lead to excessive mysticism and quirky theology. This is not to say that the Bible cannot have allegorical meaning, but to exclude a literal exegesis opens the disciple up to lots of cryptic, even arcane, philosophy.

The Pietistic Method, AKA Devotional Method, holds that the personal interpretation of the Bible outweighs what God meant to everyone in general in the plain text. In other words, they seek the deeper personal meaning of a particular portion of scripture, often to the neglect of the broader implication. The problem with this method is it can lead to egocentricity, especially if it excludes obvious meaning applicable to every believer.

It's not evil, in and of itself, because the Bible *can* be interpreted as practical in building the life of a devoted disciple—but we cannot leave out the literalness of what God was saying to the world at large.

There are, of course, other methods to hermeneutics applied to the Bible—again, this book is not to be taken as exhaustive, but to present a basic understanding of Christian doctrine. Keep the above methods in their context, each with a certain amount of fruitfulness (excepting the Rational Method, in my opinion), but ultimately finding the greatest expression in studying the Word of God *literally*.

In this is a key element to releasing the supernatural truth of God in our lives and ministries. By taking God at His black-and-white word, by not overemphasizing some deep, secret meaning, by relying upon the *logos* as inspired and infallible, by setting ourselves on a firm foundation in what God's Word teaches—we cannot, for example, but help to believe that the prayer of faith will save the sick (James 5:15) when we fully and literally interpret what the prayer of faith is, and who the sick are. Indeed, knowing the truth makes us free.

EVEN MORE TECHNICAL STUFF

Okay, you'll need to plug in for a few pages here: it's technical, but incredibly worthwhile, so kindly pay attention and underline the key stuff (I don't mind if you mark up this book; it shows you're a good student.)

Back in the '60s the late J. Edwin Hartill wrote a book called *Principles of Biblical Hermeneutics* (Zondervan: Grand Rapids) and outlined a bunch of standards that conservative evangelicals adopt when studying the Bible. I'll save you some time and briefly (ha, ha!) list them here.

- The Election Principle maintains that it is God's intention for every person in the world to be conformed to the image of Jesus Christ, and they must receive Him in order to be conformed into His image. (Romans 8:29)
- The Historical-Grammatical Principle outlines the Bible in historical, socio-political, geographical, cultural and linguistic context.
- The Dispensation (Chronometrical) Principle states God chose to deal with man's sin (and his responsibility for it) in a particular way at different times, i.e., Old Covenant, New Covenant.
- The Covenantal Principle: studying the differences of the covenants God made with His people.
- The Ethnic Division Principle: the Bible relates to three divisions of people: Jews, Gentiles and the Church.
- The Breach Principle asserts that Israel's rebellion breached their covenant with God, thereby allowing Gentiles to be engrafted in God's family.
- I'll quote the Christo-Centric Principle because it's awesome: "The mind of deity, all angelic thought and ministry, all satanic hatred and subtlety, all human hopes, the whole material universe and the entire written Word is eternally centered in Christ; therefore, all human occupation should be centered in Christ." Bam!
- The Moral Principle demands every human to have a sin nature, requiring redemption; so therefore, morality is ambiguous to unregenerate man and constant to the redeemed. That means to a born-again person there is black-and-white right and wrong. To the unsaved, morality changes from person to person. What is wrong for

one person might not be wrong for another—we call this situational ethics.

- The Discriminational Principle requires we rightly make a distinction in the Word where God makes a distinction. So if God says, "this is wrong" and "this is right"—we, too, must make that distinction.

- The Predictive Principle: prophecies have context to people at their own time and ours in future fulfillment. The prophecies of the Bible can have more than one application—to the people in the day when the word was given—to the people in the present day, there can be a spiritual application—and to people in the future.

- The Application Principle says we can only apply the truth once we've made a correct interpretation of it.

- Human Willingness means man has to *want* to understand the Bible; God does not create robots.

- The principle on Context shows that God expands on a particular subject in other passages on the same subject. So He might reference something in Genesis, expound further on it in Matthew.

Within the above principles are other sub-concepts that bear mentioning: the law of **First Mention** means pay attention to the first time a subject is mention: it's important to God.

Progressive Mention refers to subsequent thoughts expanding the First Mention throughout the Word. So find the first time "love" is mentioned in the Bible, and then read all other passages with "love" in them.

Comparative Mention means God uses parables (religious stories) and allegories (morality stories) to further a particular subject.

Complete Mention asserts God declares His full mind on any subject vital to our spiritual life; He doesn't leave the important stuff up to vagueness. If it is a topic that means heaven-or-hell or godly living on this earth, God is complete in the Bible on what He wants to say about that topic.

And now let's quickly sum up some context principles before moving on: God structures the Bible so that one passage will never contradict another; God always means what He says; certain periods of time are not commented on in the Bible; the truth of salvation is three-fold: past (justification), present (sanctification) and future (glorification); God repeats certain truths usually with additional detail; the literary structure of the Bible is perfect as God is perfect; God performs truth through illustrations of judgment; the truth is required to be tested by at least two proofs (Deuteronomy 17:6; 2 Corinthians 13:1); and lastly: the numbers, symbols and types in the Bible have meaning.

Whew! Bet your brain hurts now—I know mine does. Would all of this stuff make for a great *VeggieTales* movie, or what? Little broccolis singing about Christo-Centric, Grammatico-Historical stuff.

A LESSON FROM COWS

The Psalms use a difficultly translated Hebrew word, *selah* (Strong's #05542, "SAY-lah"), some seventy-one times. It's generally rendered to mean something like "lift up," and what we can gather about *selah* is it's probably a musical notation, referring to an instrumental interlude wherein the people are to pause singing, pondering and thinking deeply upon what was just said. To mediate on the words presented in the spiritual song. To pay attention and reflect on the intent of the singer's words. (It does *not* mean to *say, "lah!"* Sorry, bad joke...)

My friend, Chuck Flynn, has taught that *selah* means "to chew the cud;" that is, as a cow has four stomachs and must regurgitate and re-chew what it has eaten, then swallow it again, we are to "chew the cud" of the Word of God, over and over again, in deep reflection, consistently. Almost literally, we are to *digest* the Word of God at all times. Imagine all of us standing around with a deep, furrowed look in our eyes, chewing like cows. Ah, what a picture!

The purpose of studying the Word is to *renew your mind* to prove what is the only singular good, acceptable, perfect will of God (Romans 12:2) As a cow has four stomachs, there are four "chambers" to studying the Word.

The **milk of the Word** is the first chamber. (Hebrews 5:12-13) The foundations that are set forth in the Bible. (Hebrews 6:1-6) These treasures are to be hidden in our hearts. (Psalm 119:11) The purpose of memorization of scripture is to *remove dullness off your mind*. The milk of the Word lifts off that mental dullness regarding the *logos* thought of God, which in turn yields supernatural manifestation. Many people do not see the freeing truth in action because they have not digested the milk of the Word. Hebrews 6:1-6 is a correction, an admonishment: let's lay this stuff down and move beyond the milk; let's leave the discussion of these elementary principles and move on to perfection. Again, build on the foundation (progression in truth), not remain on the foundation (deterioration of truth.) But unfortunately, many of God's dear people still need the milk, and it inhibits the flow of God's miraculous truth.

The second chamber is **the washing of the water of the Word.** Ephesians 5:26 shows Jesus presenting His bride (that's us) to Himself by cleansing, sanctifying her—making her glorious and holy, without blemish, through the washing of the water of the Word. This level of studying His Word *removes debris off your mind*—that is, lifting off spiritual deadness so that you are holy and clean before your Groom.

This is the expression of the milk of the word. It is the illumination we receive from studying the water of the Word, expressed through our five senses. *Selah.*

The third chamber is the **revelation of the Word.** This third level *removes or lifts off intimidation* in expressing the authority of the Word in His name. We are now seriously digesting the milk and the water and are now able to express the milk and water to others. We are moving on to eating the meat of the Word. It is at this level that the truth of the Word is starting to be manifested (exhibiting the virtue, or power, of the *Logos.*) This is Jesus teaching in the synagogue in Mark 1:21-28. The people were *astonished* at His doctrine and *amazed* at His authority over the demonic.

Only by chewing the cud of milk (basic foundation) and water (sanctification and holy living) are we fit to eat the meat of what Jesus revealed: the power inherent in His mighty name.

The fourth and final chamber is the **image of the Word.** This final "stomach" of biblical digestion *lifts off deception,* thereby we are made to know God's own opinion of how He sees us through His Son. We are transformed (Romans 12:1-2) into the very likeness of Jesus, operating in the level of creativity that He would desire of us. This is God fulfilling our dreams through His purpose, will and desire. This is the fruit of the Spirit, not just the gifts. This is the actualization, realization of the miraculous as a permanent fixture in expression to the world. We begin to loose people out of the rudiments of fleshly living in order that they wholeheartedly serve the Lord.

This is the antithesis to the doctrine of legalism, which is simply head knowledge used to keep us worldly, fleshly, soulish in our thinking. This fourth chamber *lifts off manipulations* and moves us into the John 8:32 reference of the freedom of the truth of His Word.

The truth that sets us free is manifested into action (i.e., supernatural activity) as we *selah* the Word of God. Meditation on the *logos* is a fundamental essential for expressing a supernatural unction in our lives. Now, many philosophies teach that meditation is the *emptying* of one's mind. Christianity differs in that it teaches we are to *fill* our minds again and again with the Word of God.

> "But his delight is in the law of the Lord, and in His law he meditates day and night... My soul shall be satisfied as with marrow and fatness, and my mouth shall praise You with joyful lips. When I remember You on my bed, I meditate on You in the night watches."
>
> (Psalm 1:2; Psalm 63:5-6)

> "This Book of the Law shall not depart from your mouth, but you shall meditate in it day and night, that you may observe to do according to all that is written in it. For then you will make your way prosperous, and then you will have good success... And these words which I command you today shall be in your heart. You shall teach them diligently to your children, and shall talk of them when you sit in your house, when you walk by the way, when you lie down, and when you rise up."
>
> (Joshua 1:8; Deuteronomy 6:6-7)

Day and night, night and day, pretty much covers "always." That's right, chew your cud! Moo!

Meditation is broken down into four methods: memorization (remembering the scripture); visualization (picturing the scripture in your mind); personalization (putting your own name in the scriptures, as we did with the exegesis on 2 Thessalonians 1:3-5); and melodization (setting the scripture to music or melody.)

I don't know if melodization is a real word; melodize is, so I just added some letters, sue me.

It is important in a pursuit of freeing truth and supernatural manifestation, that we are firmly, consistently grounded in the Word of God in a literal manner. Scripture memorization, deep meditation, faith in the *logos* and in the reliability of the Bible: these are important foundations in a theology centered in the release of the miraculous. The Word of God is our nourishment, spiritual health and strength for the soul—it is even physical health for the body (see Psalm 107:17-20.) Since the Word is alive, it produces life in the believer, living faith; we are begotten by the Word of Truth and set free in the new birth—our gospel is imbued with power (Romans 1:16) to set the captives at liberty; to see they are born of incorruptible seed. (1 Peter 1:23)

The Word of God progresses us into ever-deepening expressions of the Lord's mighty power, fashioning us into warriors of truth for His kingdom.

⫫ THE TRUTH OF ⫫
HOMILETICS

Vittles. That's a really funny old word. It means victuals, provender, viands. Food. In this case, it's little, juicy niblets on how to apply hermeneutics in a cohesive fashion in order to feed others—that's what I mean by vittles. The last chapter was pretty technical, and I wanted this book to be as simplistic and entertaining as possible, but it's vitally (a play on the word vittles) important before we move on from progressing in truth to establish a concrete foundation on the importance of the Word and the correct interpretation of it. I'm convinced this solves 95% of Christians' problems concerning a hindrance to seeing the power of God flow in their lives: simply not knowing the truth that makes them free, or misinterpreting that truth.

So I want to take a few pages to expand upon the truth of studying God's Word by supplying a couple nuggets (another food metaphor, I must be hungry!) on implementing hermeneutics in an intelligent, organized fashion. Even if you don't "preach to the masses," these principles can be applied in your daily studying of God's Word to benefit your knowledge of the truth.

We call this *homiletics*, from the Greek (there they are again!) *homilos* (Strong's #3658, "HOM-ee-loss"), meaning "people together, a crowd," and from *homilia* (Strong's #3657, "hom-ih-LEE-uh"), which means "communication," or for our purpose, "a sermon." So, the science of preaching, composing a homily. Preaching is an act of worship; it must be, otherwise the congregation may worship the preacher and not God.

One thing I've noticed over the years, and I'm not being critical here, just pointing out an observation; but it seems there's been a marked decline in people behind the pulpit having a homiletically sound sermon, and it's because of this lack of structured teaching that some strange notions are taught to the people. So one of the primary things I taught my students when I lectured in Bible colleges was the importance of hermeneutics and homiletics.

(I'm not meaning the above as a blanket statement, that all teaching should be rigid or legalistic in development—just that there should be some concise, coherent train of thought behind the spoken word. Many preachers only preach in "one-liners," and too many one-liners can cause confusion, because the concepts are not flushed out enough.)

It's probably just that many people simply don't know how to compile a compelling, doctrinal message, or perhaps some people feel it will stifle the "free move" of the Spirit. However, it's been my experience that it is exactly the opposite—teaching a well thought-out word creates an atmosphere for the Spirit to move.

A key to supernatural release in manifesting the truth is found in rightly dividing the Word (again, 2 Timothy 2:15), to convey properly the subject matter of the Bible in the entirety of its context.

In other words, don't just take one or two scriptures on, say, the blood of Jesus—but study the *entirety* of the Scripture on the subject of the blood of Jesus, the Old Testament types and foreshadows in light of the New Testament revelation on the preciousness of His blood, from Genesis 3:21 to Revelation 19:13. The Bible is meant to be studied topically not just subjectively, from cover to cover, in order to get the full mind of God on a particular theme.

This goes back to the context principles in the previous chapter. Context means "woven together," connecting a thought throughout the whole of the passage.

It's been taught there are two methods of context of which the writers of the Bible were used to convey the *logos* of God.

One, the "Fresh Revelation Context" is where the Spirit inspired new concepts to the writers of which they previously didn't know anything about. Since the Spirit inspired the words, obviously He must interpret them, for the writers and for the readers.

Two, the "Woven Revelation Context" is where the Spirit inspired concepts of the *logos* that were woven together (contextually) with concepts already known to the writer. So, when Scripture authors quote other Scripture authors, this is woven context. It also indicates that the **Spirit uses the Bible to interpret the Bible.** The Word of God is the best source for interpreting the Word of God. That is a key component to a homiletic teaching.

Theologians call this the "hermeneutical circle": the parts can never be understood without the whole; and in support of exegesis, the whole can never be understood without understanding its parts. Wow, that can be confusing if you read it too fast!

1 Corinthians 2:13 alludes to this: the Holy Ghost teaches fresh revelation, and comparing the spiritual truths with spiritual language (see the Amplified Bible) connotes woven context.

To be homiletically sound, all Scripture must be interpreted in proper context, meaning an individual verse should be read in light of the passage surrounding it. Moving out larger, that passage should be read in light of the entire book. Then larger in scope, the book should be read in light of the Testament it is in (Old or New.) And lastly, the Testament itself should be read in the context of the whole Bible.

See why being diligent in studying the Word is so vittley (I misspelled that on purpose) important? If you read what was above, that means a verse should be applied throughout the entirety of the Bible itself—not on its own.

One important key here I want to drive home: **the New Testament interprets the Old.** Every bit of the OT (the Era of Law) must be correctly interpreted through the NT (the Era of Grace.) This does *not* negate the OT in the slightest. Rather, the completion and perfection of the OT is found in the fulfillment of Jesus Christ in the NT. Every type, symbol, poem, prophecy and law of the OT finds its ultimate satisfaction in the Lord Himself—that's why He *is* the *Logos*; it's all about Him!

Let me offer you a bit of friendly advice: when you study the Word of God, *live in the gospels and the epistles.*

What I mean by that is no one, no one, no one taught the *logos* better than the *Logos* taught about Himself. Jesus, the greatest preacher, the most homiletically sound, hermeneutically unassailable, prophetically accurate, Spiritually inspired Man in history was infallible in His revelation of what the Bible means: He was perfection incarnate.

If you never taught out of anything else than the first four books of the New Testament, you could never exhaust the resources that they expound in your ministry.

Living in the gospels, living in His sermons and parables, will never lead you down a funky path of strange teaching and preaching. Secondarily, the epistles, mainly written by Paul who received his doctrine directly from Jesus Christ, execute every facet of righteous living we can be concerned with.

The rest of the Bible should be contextually interpreted through these two avenues: what does Jesus say in the gospels and what do the apostles say in the epistles. Take any contentious teaching you've ever heard, boil it down through these two paths, and you'll come out all right.

If these two roads are silent on the subject, don't teach it behind the pulpit. Pay attention to what I just said. If Christ or the apostles don't comment on a particular subject—don't make a sermon of it behind the pulpit. This will save you a lot of trouble!

Use the Law (I mean, the Pentateuch or first five books of the Bible: Genesis, Exodus, Leviticus, Numbers, Deuteronomy) to find the completion of itself (the Law) in faith through Christ's redemptive works. Use the Historical Books (Joshua through Esther) to study the context of Jewish history in light of the advent of the Messiah; the execution of the Old Covenant and its subsequent breach by the Israelites.

Use the Poetical Books (Job through Song of Solomon) for daily living; use the Psalms for inspiration; use Proverbs and Ecclesiastes for wisdom; use Job when your faith is being tested. Use the major prophets (Isaiah through Daniel) to see the fulfillment of prophecy found in Christ and the future of His kingdom through us. Use the minor prophets (Hosea through Malachi) for the historical context of finding Jesus as the Messiah of the Jews and God's judgment on those who neglect His covenant with Him.

All of these should be represented in the context of the Gospels/Historical Books (Matthew-Acts) firstly; the Pauline Epistles (Romans through Philemon) secondly; and the so-called "Non-Pauline" Epistles (Hebrews through Revelation) thirdly. I say "so-called" because Hebrews is argued by many to be of Pauline authorship.

By firstly, secondly, thirdly, I don't mean one is less important than the other, just that the teachings of Jesus as portrayed in the gospels should always be given a position of preeminence concerning doctrinal dispute. Paul is given "preeminence" only in the sense of his writing the bulk of the New Testament, not that Peter and the others were of any less importance in being inspired by the Holy Spirit.

(You know, I recall a very well-known preacher saying he had to repent of living in the epistles more than the gospels, because he found he was loving the words of Paul more than the words of Jesus.)

THE NATURE OF PREACHING

"For since, in the wisdom of God, the world through wisdom did not know God, it pleased God by the foolishness of the message preached to save those who believe." (1 Corinthians 1:21)

> "How then shall they call on Him in whom they have not believed? And how shall they believe in Him of whom they have not heard? And how shall they hear without a preacher?"
> (Romans 10:14)

"...Who exchanged the truth of God for the lie, and worshiped and served the creature rather than the Creator, who is blessed forever. Amen." (Romans 1:25)

The purpose of preaching is to communicate the truth of God to meet the needs of the people. As Proverbs 23:23 says, "Buy the truth, and do not sell it, also wisdom and instruction and understanding." It's a stock that can only go up in value.

As preachers and teachers of the Word of Truth, it's important we remain culturally sensitive to the people we are preaching and teaching to—to know where they lack so we can apply the truth to their needs. Homiletics helps us build a better word for the people to whom it is intended, to help them understand the truth in God's Word.

> "And Ezra opened the book in the sight of all the people, for he was standing above all the people; and when he opened it, all the people stood up. And Ezra blessed the Lord, the great God. Then all the people answered, 'Amen, Amen!' while lifting up their hands. And they bowed their heads and worshiped the Lord with their faces to the ground. Also... Jeshua, Bani, Sherebiah, Jamin, Akkub, Shabbethai, Hodijah, Maaseiah, Kelita, Azariah, Jozabad, Hanan, Pelaiah, and the Levites, helped the people to understand the Law; and the people stood in their place. So they read distinctly from the book, in the Law of God; and they gave the sense, and helped them to understand the reading."
>
> (Nehemiah 8:5-8)

Your sermons should be biblical, and by that I mean the concepts presented should be harmonious with the original intent of the authors of the Scripture. The point of a sermon is to change the audience's behavior on a particular subject: to move them to action, revealing God's truth so that they are stirred to live the life that God has called them to live.

Homiletics teaches there are basically three kinds of sermons: topical, textual (also called exegetical) and expository.

To preach topically is to preach on a particular subject independently of the scriptural text. This means your main point comes from several passages of scripture that outline and support one topic, like say, "salvation" or "love."

A textual/exegetical sermon takes its main points directly from one particular passage, usually even one verse, in the Bible. Here you dissect the actual passage, line upon line, to draw out the meaning. So, for example, you take John 3:16 and make a salvation message out of it. What does it mean, "For God so loved the world?"

Expository preaching exposes (clever!) a particular passage, usually several verses, possibly from different parts of the Bible, and interprets that passage in relation to the author's intent. What that means is the material of the sermon is taken directly from the text in the Bible and discusses a series of concepts around one main idea. So, for an example, if you take Galatians 5:16-26, you outline what Paul means by "works of the flesh" opposed to "fruit of the Spirit."

Someone, somewhere, sometime once skillfully stated: "Topical is preaching *about* the Bible, textual is preaching *from* the Bible, and expository is preaching *the* Bible."

Homiletically speaking, every sermon you preach should contain the same similar structure. Every sermon needs a catchy *title*, something interesting, dignified, short and to the point. It should sum up what you're going to share. So, something like, "The Peculiar People." Or, "Why do Christians suffer?" Or, "Take up your cross!"

The *text* is the scripture(s) that make up the subject of your message. You should always clearly define your text and read it aloud carefully. In secular presentations, this is the *thesis*.

Your message should have an *introduction*. Something brief, entertaining that gets the listeners' attention and builds a rapport between you and them, leading into the main part of the sermon.

The *main principles* order the homily. Keys to remember are clarity and unity. The generally accepted rule is to have at least three main points and no more than five. Each principle should clearly add upon the previous point, developing the complete thought; the principles should be plainly distinct from each other, and they should flow logically in order.

Illustrations are important to highlight the message you are trying to convey by sharing examples. They help the listeners grasp the truth you're trying to share; they can be from your own experience, from the Bible—like parables, or from someone else's experience, but they should be well-cited and verifiable, otherwise it's called "hearsay."

Lastly, every good sermon needs a powerful *conclusion*. This is a climatic statement, summing up the main points, to drive the concept home. It should be simple and positive, pulling at the heartstrings of your listeners, and every conclusion requires a "call to action"—what are you expecting your audience to do?

So, let's summarize and move on:

- Title
- Text
- Introduction
- Main Points
- Illustrations
- Conclusion

REVEAL, ILLUMINATE, INTERPRET

Do you feel like you're in school again? Hopefully not quite so boring! But I really feel, in a book on basic fundamentals, it is important at least to highlight the need for hermeneutical study and homiletic sermon prep. Even if you're not a preacher or teacher, say, just someone who gets up to share a testimony in front of the congregation: these principles apply to every Christian.

Now before we leave this classroom, let's tie this into a release of the supernatural, as I am writing a book on truth warriors, not just technical practicalities.

It is my firm persuasion that the Lord never intended His disciples (that's us) to teach or preach or give testimony from His Word without some kind of sign and wonder to back up the authority of that Word. The Lord has graciously permitted me to preach for nearly four decades now (whew!) I have always prayed and asked that He back up the word I share with some kind of supernatural expression that proves the validity biblically of what I just said. I didn't just want to share a fancy word and not see the people moved by the Dancing Hand of God. This is not to say that some ministers don't have a supernatural unction behind their teaching and preaching—the word they share itself can be supernatural in its delivery, and the congregation is changed. But the point is: we as truth warriors should always be anticipating some kind of evident token that the Lord's approval is on what we just preached, taught or shared.

So if I give a sermon on, say, faith, I ask the Lord to impart a supernatural expression of faith to the people who just heard the word. If I teach on healing, I want to see people healed by His authority and grace. I don't think it's wrong to expect the Lord to back up His Word when it's shared in a scripturally sound way. See why diligence in hermeneutics and homiletics would be so important?

"Then the Lord said to me, 'You have seen well, for I am ready to perform My word.'" (Jeremiah 1:12)

God watches over His Word to perform it. We, as His mouthpieces on this earth, are utilized by Him to ensure the word we share—if it is in line with *His* Word—will produce the desired effect. That tells me something. If we're not witnessing His Word being performed, we just might not be sharing it correctly. We have not "seen well." That's not meant to be a critique, just an observation. We *should* be anticipating the Lord to stand behind His own Word, since it's placed above His name (again, Psalm 138:2.)

> "So shall My word be that goes forth from My mouth; it shall not return to Me void, but it shall accomplish what I please, and it shall prosper in the thing for which I sent it."
>
> (Isaiah 55:11)

The point is, we as truth warriors, always seeking that expression of God's supernatural virtue, must align our words with His Word, so that it's not returned void and unprosperous (I think that's a made up word, but I like it.) If there is no supernatural authority to prove the word, it's not on Him—because:

"God is not a man, that He should lie, nor a son of man, that He should repent. Has He said, and will He not do? Or has He spoken, and will He not make it good?" (Numbers 23:19)

The question resides with us: have we said what He's said? Have we spoken what He's spoken? Because if we're not seeing Him do something we expect, or make good on something we think He should, it's possible we're not speaking forth what He's spoken; we're not saying the things He's said. And therefore, He's under no obligation to "make good" on something that didn't originate from His mouth.

That's why a firm foundation in His Word, what these past three chapters have been driving at, is so wholly, *vittley* important!

Here's one of those instances I prefer the Old King James over the New: "Study to shew thyself approved unto God, a workman that needeth not to be ashamed, rightly dividing the word of truth." (2 Timothy 2:15, KJV)

So be good disciples: study to show yourself approved, rightly divide that word of truth, then you'll see the Word back Himself up!

See, the brain is a fascinating machine. It works systematically and creatively to organize and structure thoughts. Thoughts are images, and images become words. Follow me here? The brain's a very fast computer! But this is also the problem. Without a methodical system of interpretation, our own minds get in the way of seeing a release of God's anointing. Our minds must be renovated to interpret what God has said accurately and truthfully.

We know that God's glory resides in our spirits; we are the temple of the Holy Ghost (see 1 Corinthians 6:19.) It is from there that all revelation of God originates. He *reveals* Himself, His *logos*, to our spirits, because He is a Spirit.

"God is Spirit, and those who worship Him must worship in spirit and truth." (John 4:24)

The key is to get the glory of God residing in our spirits out from our minds and through our five senses. In essence, what this means is the Holy Spirit must *illuminate* our minds to interpret properly what is being revealed from the glory-realm of God. This is *rhema* when studying the Word.

There are areas of our minds, all of us, that are "darkened," that is, not in agreement with our spirit-man, what we know to be God's truth, that the Holy Spirit must renew, that is, illuminate (again, see Romans 12:2.) The mark of a mature believer is one, who through the washing of the water of the Word, has had his or her mind renewed, thus discerning good from evil.

"But solid food belongs to those who are of full age, that is, those who by reason of use have their senses exercised to discern both good and evil." (Hebrews 5:14)

Notice it is the senses that the author of Hebrews is saying must be exercised, just like any other muscle in our body that responds to application. The meat of the Word is only for those who have worked out (had illuminated) those senses to discern what is of God and what is not of God.

This is the act of *interpretation*: taking the revelation that has been illuminated and exercising it through our five senses to release the glory.

Illumination is for *you* personally to cotton on to the revelation. Interpretation is for *them*, others, at least after a fashion in the context of this teaching. It comes out of your spirit-man through thoughts in your sanctified mind, which are images, and we know images become words, out through your body, through your physical mouth.

Really take a moment to understand the above statement. Our words must originate from the spirit-man. The revelation from *the* Spirit is *illuminated* within *your* spirit, becoming thoughts in your mind, which you in turn make into words, and share the *interpretation* with others. From the Spirit through the spirit out through the body.

Without getting too deep here, what I'm simply saying is interpretation is the truth expressed to other people.

> "You are our epistle written in our hearts, known and read by all men; clearly you are an epistle of Christ, ministered by us, written not with ink but by the Spirit of the living God, not on tablets of stone but on tablets of flesh, that is, of the heart."
>
> (2 Corinthians 3:2-3)

We become living epistles. In a fashion, the Lord is represented through us—just as He is the *Logos* of God made flesh, we are *His logos* made flesh. This is the release of the supernatural, the glory of God manifest in the earth through vessels of clay.

"But we have this treasure in earthen vessels, that the excellence of the power may be of God and not of us." (2 Corinthians 4:7)

This is why hermeneutics and homiletics are significant in the life of a truth warrior. No matter if we preach, teach, or give testimony simply as lay people, the principles are the same. The pure revelation, the glory, can only be expressed from an illuminated mind that has correctly interpreted that revelation. If we cannot understand, we cannot have faith for the supernatural truth of God to be manifested.

This is why some people can sit in a dynamic service with signs, wonders and miracles and still leave dull: their minds, at least in certain areas, are unilluminated (I am *so* good at making up these words!) This is a major reason for seeing a *lack* of the supernatural, the truth being displayed.

Some people may think hermeneutical study is "boring" or a homiletic sermon is "religious." But the facts don't lie: God does nothing apart from His Word. It is His complete *logos* that stands forever.

"Heaven and earth will pass away, but My words will by no means pass away." (Matthew 24:35; Mark 13:31)

This was the *Logos* speaking of His *logos*. A supernatural expression in our lives is directly related to our level of *knowing* Christ as the *Logos*. I'll say it again, it is the truth you know that makes you free. The way to know Truth (John 14:6) is to study His *logos* and properly interpret it. Christ always backed up what He preached with a supernatural flow of anointing that cleansed the lepers, healed the sick, raised the dead, showing He was the Way, the Truth and the Life. And guess what, dear students of the Word, no one comes unto the Father but through the Word!

☵ THE TRUTH OF ☵ THE TRINITY

All right. That was some good stuff in the previous chapters, if I do say so myself. I hope you enjoyed reading it as much as I enjoyed writing it. But more than that, I hope it added an element of *truth* to your warriorness (made up word!) I trust a deeper doctrinal truth was engrafted in your theology on just how important the Bible is, how to study it correctly and how to teach it properly.

Since this next section deals specifically with theology (the study of God), it makes the most sense to move into a discussion on the Trinity first, the revelation of truth that is found in the Father, Son and Holy Spirit as one God in three distinct Persons. From there we'll break it down more fully.

Now, I'm not really sure why this is such a touchy subject among many Christians, or why it's considered such a difficult concept to grasp. I think the Bible is exceptionally clear on the Triune God. But I think where the hardships come are from people placing either a) too much emphasis on the One God; or b) too much emphasis on the Three God (no, I didn't forget to put an "s" there); or c) too much emphasis on the three "Gods," if that makes sense.

There is an awful lot of quirkiness (believe it or not, that's a real word!) on the concept of the Trinity that has led to major heresy throughout the centuries and an appalling amount of division that God never intended for His people to deal with. To Him, it's not that difficult, and He revealed Himself rather well in His Word. However, that's the key point: it is only through careful hermeneutical study that we remain stable and correct in our doctrine concerning the God we worship.

That's why chapters like this are so important in doctrine books. Some people will not like me for this, and that's okay. I believe this doctrine is "fair and balanced" concerning the oneness of God and the threeness (so made up!) of God, just like the Manness of Jesus and the Godness of Jesus you'll read in just a bit. We cannot place too much emphasis on either or, but both!

It is important when discussing three-in-one and one-in-three (sounds like Musketeers) that we are very careful not to spill over on one side to the exclusion of the other—this is how heresy is created, and this is what has mucked up the concept of a triune, singular God in ways He never intended.

A Christian cannot divide God into three, because He is undividable—if the Christian tries, this becomes Tritheism, the worship of three Gods separately.

A Christian cannot combine God because He is distinctively represented in three Persons—if the Christian tries, this becomes Unitarianism, the worship of a numerically one (1) God.

Whenever we as Christians study the threeness of God, it must be in light of the oneness of God, and vice versa, based on the entirety of God's *logos* about Himself.

All right. Where to begin? Let's give some definitions for the word "God" (or the lack thereof), and expand on them. Acts, Romans and Colossians talk about "Godhead," which is often quoted in people's statements of faith. Something akin to, "We believe in one eternal Godhead..." Or sometimes, "We believe in one God, eternally represented in three Persons, distinct but inseparable..." Something like that.

–ISMS

Monotheism (incidentally, this chapter will use a lot of –isms) is the belief in one God. The major monotheistic religions of the world are Christianity, Judaism, Islam. And really, let's take a step back for a second and ponder this concept. Can there really be many gods? Does this even make sense? Maybe it's just me, but even before I was born-again, the concept of more than one God means there isn't *God*—THE supreme Being—just many "almost-gods" or "lesser gods" all trying to get one up on Zeus, or whoever. That just sounds like normal *people* to me. Seems silly. At least, that's the way it works in my brain.

But who am I, right? Pantheism—many gods—is championed by major world religions (Hinduism, Buddhism—sort of—Shinto, Wicca, Animism—technically, although Animists would argue otherwise) and most mythologies of the ancient world (Greek, Roman, Celtic, and so on), inclusive of ancestral worship.

Now, technically, Catholicism rejects the "worship" of saints and maintains there is only one God represented in Trinity. However, place the emphasis on "technically." Having *technically* grown up Catholic, whenever we *did* go to Mass (hardly ever), I found the people, even the clergy, placed just as much emphasis on Mary and the saints as the Lord Himself.

There are varying levels of pantheism (Hinduism has some 300 million gods), but it's tedious to go into, and doesn't really matter anyway, since pantheism is a confusing waste of time. So let's get even more silly, shall we? (Smiley face goes here.)

Atheism means "no god." Forms of atheism can be practical (professing there is no god) or theoretical (acting like there is no god) in application.

In my experience, I've never met a true atheist. They claim to be, but really, to be an atheist, one must have exhausted *every* religion in the world, and then come to the conclusion there still is no god. To say there is no God and not have studied that concept out exhaustively seems foolish in the extreme.

Really, in my mind, atheism is just a form of laziness. And it is true, many people go to hell, not so much because they're such terrible people—it's because of laziness; they don't comprehensively seek out an answer.

Agnosticism is "there may be a god, or maybe not." It is the height of ignorance, since agnostic means, "I cannot know."

Trinitarianism Christianity is unique in proclaiming one God represented in three distinct Persons (Islam and Judaism unequivocally reject this notion—obviously.) While some divisions of Christianity believe there is just one God—this is called Unitarianism, nontrinitarianism or oneness—the quote-unquote mainstream of Christianity believe in the Trinity (Catholic and Protestant alike.)

Some common nontrinitarianism Christian movements are Unitarian Universalist Christians, Bible Students (Millennialist Restorationists), Christadelphians, Christian Scientists, *Iglesia ni Cristo*, Jehovah's Witnesses, certain Latter Day Saint movements (not all), Oneness Pentecostals, and the United Church of God.

Some –isms regarding Unitarianism are Arianism (not Aryanism—that's Nazism), Adoptionism, Modalism and Monarchianism. Some dude named Arius about three hundred years after Christ ascended, taught that there was only one God, the Father, and He created the Son as some kind of *Star Wars*-ian Anakin Skywalker, a super-angel, who in turn created the Spirit, which I guess would be like... Yoda or something. (Perhaps I'm oversimplifying.)

Adoptionism maintains that Jesus was "adopted" by the Father as the Son at His baptism, thus implying He was not pre-incarnate as deity. Almost sort of like Jesus became a demigod, a human raised to godlike status by the Father's adoption.

Monarchianism maintains there is just one God—the monarch of all creation.

Modalism is sometimes called Sabellianism after another dude named Sabellius taught that God is one Person, but He sometimes operates in different modes as the Son, or the Spirit, or the Father, and essentially is talking to Himself in the Bible. It's like His first name, middle name and last name, or whatever. Like He gave birth to Himself, and then anointed Himself to redeem people to Himself, through Himself. I don't know, it's confusing.

So before we delve into this God *we're* talking about, let's set up a few more concepts when we use the word "God."

God must be Love (loving), blameless, virtuous, moral, holy, just, merciful, trustworthy and benevolent (see Leviticus 19:2; Deuteronomy 32:4; 1 John 4:8 as just a few citings.) God is an invisible Spirit and is perceived or "seen" spiritually. (John 4:24) God is Light, absolutely pure and indestructible, incorruptible, indivisible; His glory is beyond human description. (1 John 1:5) God must be all-powerful, all-knowing, all-present, self-sufficient, self-existing, apart and outside the parameters of His creation (this earthly plane, outer space, the cosmos and time.) God does not need anything from anyone ever to sustain Himself. If everything else ceased to be, He still would be. He exists in the past, present, future simultaneously—it is all the same to Him; there is no time apart from as He wills it, since He is the one who created it. There is nothing He does not know, and there is nothing He cannot do, for to be deceitful implies the ability to change.

He can create something from nothing just by a sheer act of will—in this case, speaking forth, as in, "Let there be." (Genesis 1:3) Nothing has life apart from Him. (John 5:26)

To be anything less is to be *not* God. So there is God, and then there is everything else. He is above and apart from everything; there is nothing above Him. He is *El Elyon* (see Strong's #5945, "el-YOWN"; Genesis 14:18; Psalm 57:2), God the Most High, God the Highest. He has always been before there was a "been" and will always be even when there is no more "be." That is what God means when He says His name is "I AM," which—I don't know about you—but I think that is a *very* cool name.

See why it's silly to believe in many gods? How can they all be "the only One"?

THREENESS AND ONENESS

There is only one God who exists in three Persons, distinctly discernable, yet entirely inseparable. What this means is, when you get to heaven, you will see a spirit Being sitting on a throne called Father; you will see another Being in a glorified body called Son; you will see another spirit Being called Spirit. They are distinct in threeness and can be "seen" (spiritually) as individual; yet Their essence, Their eternal makeup, is singular in oneness, of the same substance and worth—They are one God, one in unity, one in importance, one in thought and deed; three in expression or manifestation. All three are one God and are of the same equal value and power. They cannot exist apart from the other, any more than you could exist apart from your brain, heart and lungs. God is distinct but undividable. Never has one unharmonious instance ever occurred between God, not one disconcordant breath; nor can there be, for God is one and is inseparable. All are God, the only God, worthy of being worshipped as God, because what else do you do with God but worship Him?

The Son is not less than the Father (He is begotten, not born or created), nor the Spirit less than the Son. Jesus sent us "Another" of the same kind as Himself—God. (John 14:16; 15:26) The Spirit glorifies and testifies of the Son, the Son glorifies and testifies of the Father, and in turn the Father glorifies and testifies of the Son and the Spirit. All authority in heaven and earth is given to the Son, executed by the Spirit, for glory to the Father. All three instantly and always work in perfect unison (oneness; "uni" means "one.")

When we pray to God, it is not blasphemy to pray to the Son in His name as God, in the power of the Spirit as God, to access the Father as God. Some people teach it's wrong to pray to the Father directly, or to pray to Jesus as God Himself, or to worship the Spirit as God Himself—but it is through the Son and the Spirit that we have a right to call God "Father." (Romans 8:15; Galatians 4:6—the Trinity in action!)

Both the Old and New Testaments testify (clever!) that there is Father God, Son God (the Word), Holy Spirit God, and that They are one in complete and total trinity (tri-unity, "tri" means three, "uni" again means "one," "ty" means "together"—I mean, I'm speaking simply here for clarity, but break the word down.)

Genesis 1:1-2 uses the word *Elohiym* (Strong's #430, "el-oh-HEEM"), and it is a plural of the word *Elowahh* (Strong's #433, "el-OH-ah") which is the long form of *El* (Strong's #410, "ALE.") *El* means "God," describing "might, strength and power."

(Dante's *De vulgari eloquentia* talks about *El* being the first sound Adam made, the joy at recognizing his Creator—kind of a neat thought, utterly unsupported by scripture, but cool nonetheless.)

Elohiym means "God" in the plural intensive with a singular meaning. It means one plural. Sounds weird, huh?

Some oneness believers argue that *Elohiym* is simply the superlative degree of the singular, kind of like taking a singular and making it plural to add extreme emphasis to it. Officially this is called *pluralis excellentiae.*

Nowadays, we'd just add –est to the end of the word, like, "the mostest, bestest." But in olden days, they would pluralize the singular to make it accentuated; hence, similar to the royal "we"—myself and my majesty, "us, ourself." (That's called *pluralis majestatis.*)

Is it just me, but doesn't that cheapen God to sound schizophrenic? Perhaps all my students in England don't have a problem with Her Majesty's Majesty talking about "our royal self." I don't know. But it sounds odd to my American ear!

In any case, God referring to Himself in the third person cheapens the whole experience of the Bible, and is totally contradictory to the entirety of the *logos*. "Let us make man in our image," He says to Himself. (Genesis 1:26) Huh?

I suppose some argue He was talking to the host of heaven, the angelic beings, except the angelic host didn't have any more activity or power in the creation of man than did the animal kingdom. In other words, God did not ask the angels' help to make man.

Nor did the angels have the same kind of God's life within them, as Adam did. God's Spirit resides in the angelic in an entirely different manner than within us. This is why we are not related to angels any more than we are related to the animal kingdom (I mean, made in the animals' image.) So it's kind of ridiculous to assume we're made in the angels' image, which would be the logical inference of reading "man in our image" if God was speaking to His heavenly host.

From cover to cover, the Bible reveals God as one and God as three, not emphasizing one state of being over the other, just in perfect equilibrium. You want scriptures, don't you? Good!

You've been paying attention to the point of this book! So, here we go:

Deuteronomy 6:4 states, "Hear, O Israel: the Lord our God, the Lord is one!"

Isaiah 48:16 points out the Father, the Spirit and the Son, each distinct, in one verse: "Come near to Me, hear this: I have not spoken in secret from the beginning; from the time that it was, I was there. And now the Lord God and His Spirit have sent Me."

(The Hebrew verb "have" is singular, as in the Lord God and His Spirit "has" sent Me, yet two distinct subjects are present in the sentence: the Lord God and His Spirit; and They "has" sent Jesus, not Themselves or each Other.)

Psalm 86:10: "For You are great, and do wondrous things; You alone are God." He stands alone as God: the only One.

Isaiah again points out the Trinity in distinction:

> "The Spirit of the Lord God is upon Me, because the Lord has anointed Me to preach good tidings to the poor; He has sent Me to heal the brokenhearted, to proclaim liberty to the captives, and the opening of the prison to those who are bound..."
>
> (Isaiah 61:1)

The Spirit was upon the Son because the Father anointed Jesus. To isolate the subjects of this verse, or to unify this verse as numerically one Being, is not only impractical and insensible; but demeans and works against the entire redemptive acts of Jesus, operating under the authority of the Father, by the power of the Spirit.

This is why the Trinity is so important to you and me as truth warriors of the supernatural. Splitting the oneness of God or negating the threeness of God is a danger to His supernatural expression through the Godhead!

"No one is holy like the Lord, for there is none besides You, nor is there any rock like our God." (1 Samuel 2:2)

None besides God once again points out His oneness as the one and only God. The Jews of the Old Testament were monotheistic as opposed to the polytheistic Gentiles around them. However, they also recognized that the Lord God, Father, would send His Son, a distinct Person of the Godhead.

Psalm 110:1 is written by the psalmist king, speaking of the LORD God and his (David's) Lord as two distinct persons (the Father and the Son.) "The LORD said to my Lord, 'Sit at My right hand, till I make Your enemies Your footstool.'"

Without understanding of a triune God, the intent—and even the coherence—of this statement is lost. "The Lord said to Himself, come sit by Myself at My own right hand until I make My enemies My own footstool..."

See, I've confused myself already.

Some Unitarians argue God is speaking of an earthly lord that would follow David, not necessarily the Messiah. Except the Father God is speaking about a Priest forever after the order of Melchizedek, and Hebrews 5 and 7 blatantly point out this is referring to the Son of God, Jesus Christ. Hence the reason the modern NKJ translation capitalizes all of the "Your's" in the Psalm. Even Jesus Himself pointed out the absurdity of this notion in Matthew 22:41-46.

The New Testament further expands the truth of the Trinity, keeping devoted to the OT purity of monotheism expressed in three distinct Persons.

"Jesus answered him, 'The first of all the commandments is: "Hear, O Israel, the Lord our God, the Lord is one. And you shall love the Lord your God with all your heart, with all your soul, with all your mind, and with all your strength." This is the first commandment. And the second, like it, is this: "You shall love your neighbor as yourself." There is no other commandment greater than these.' So the scribe said to Him, 'Well said, Teacher. You have spoken the truth, for there is one God, and there is no other but He.'"

(Mark 12:29-32)

"And I will pray the Father, and He will give you another Helper, that He may abide with you forever—the Spirit of truth, whom the world cannot receive, because it neither sees Him nor knows Him; but you know Him, for He dwells with you and will be in you."

(John 14:16-17)

Jesus recognized the oneness of the Godhead, and the three-ness of the Godhead. Obviously in the excerpt from John, it's an absurdity to equate that Jesus was praying to Himself to send another Himself. To assume that Jesus was referring to a numerically singular One, all inclusive of Himself, the Father and the Spirit as the same Entity, is to assume that Jesus thought the people were too ignorant to understand the concept of a triune God, and therefore, He was being purposefully illusory in order that they might "get it."

This is the same notion in saying that Jesus wasn't actually casting out physical demons when He ministered deliverance, but merely that the people were too superstitious (and stupid) to "get it," so that Jesus was referring to mental/physical oppressions and vexations as spiritually fallen beings. Again, this means that Jesus was intentionally deceiving (or let's soften that and say *misleading*) the people He came to enlighten. Silliness.

To ignore the Trinity of the one God is to say He deliberately misinforms His people because they're not smart enough to understand. I know that's a strong statement, and I truly love those Christians that are oneness in philosophy, but can you see how important this concept of Trinity is to truth warriors? We cannot ignore the threeness in light of the oneness, any more than we can place the oneness over the threeness. Not either or, both!

"Now a mediator does not mediate for one only, but God is one." (Galatians 3:20)

God is indeed One, but here's a perfect scripture for the oneness and threeness of God from the same author, Paul:

> "There are diversities of gifts, but the same Spirit. There are differences of ministries, but the same Lord. And there are diversities of activities, but it is the same God who works all in all."
> (1 Corinthians 12:4-6)

The Spirit is the Spirit (duh), the Lord is Jesus Christ, God is the Father, each with diverse gifts, ministries and activities, all in the same God working all in all. Now, if Paul was strictly oneness, why make the distinction between the three? Just say, there is one (numerically) God who gives different gifts, ministers in diverse ways, through various actions. Why show God as three distinct manifestations if it's only the operations that are distinct? Yet Paul makes it very clear it is the same God—each Person is unified God.

> "I, therefore, the prisoner of the Lord, beseech you to walk worthy of the calling with which you were called, with all lowliness and gentleness, with longsuffering, bearing with one another in love, endeavoring to keep the unity of the Spirit in the bond of peace. There is one body and one Spirit, just as you were called in one hope of your calling; one Lord, one faith, one baptism; one God and Father of all, who is above all, and through all, and in you all."
>
> (Ephesians 4:1-6)

My goodness, what eloquence! Thank you, Paul! But boy, that's a lot of ones. And yet, I find three separate manifestations of deity. A Spirit, a Lord and a Father, yet he says one God. Three-in-One. Was Paul misinforming the church at Ephesus?

"You believe that there is one God. You do well. Even the demons believe—and tremble!" (James 2:19)

Hey, even the demonic knows there is only one God. And it scares the daylights out of them!

"For through Him we both have access by one Spirit to the Father." (Ephesians 2:18)

Here's Paul again trying to confuse those poor Ephesians. One Person providing access to one Person through one Person, but they're all the same People? No, it doesn't make sense to me either.

> "For there are three that bear witness in heaven: the Father, the Word, and the Holy Spirit; and these three are one. And there are three that bear witness on earth: the Spirit, the water, and the blood; and these three agree as one."
>
> (1 John 5:7-8)

The above verse contains the controversial Comma Johanneum; it is present in the King James versions and others, but several translations leave it out, or add it to the footnotes, as of questionable authenticity, meaning they're not sure if it was originally written by John.

For five centuries people have been arguing the validity, or lack thereof, of including the portion of the passage that refers to the Trinity. Whatever the case, it isn't likely that the debates will be settled until Christ returns to set us all straight. While most—not all—scholars don't think it was "nefariously" added by some scribe who was pro-Trinity, those who are against the clause's inclusion generally chalk it up to a "gloss" (meant as a marginal explanation), and not from the pen (or is that quill?) of John himself.

To me, it's really an unnecessary argument regarding proof/non-proof of the Trinity, since many other scriptures refer to a Triune God. So, in my eyes, it's more for the academics to have something to argue about, and not to prove or disprove the Trinity—unless one really believes the "addition" was infamously added to sway non-Trinitarians.

Not that anyone cares, but my personal belief is it should be included. For now, let's move on to some "ones."

ARGUMENTS OF "ONE"

So, there are two different words used in the OT and NT that are translated "one," but they have distinctive meanings. (I'll get to these in a moment, but let's build the suspense.)

For these different words, the basic concept is, in English, saying I have one apple. That is numerically one (1) apple. Not two apples, just one, singular apple. And then saying you and I are in one mind and one accord (Philippians 2:2); no, we don't share the same mind—you and I each have our own minds that are in perfect unity (plural one.)

I have one sock—who knows why, I lost the other one. The point is there is a single, solitary sock (1) all by its stinky lonesome. But my wife and I are one flesh. (Genesis 2:24) Not really, I have my own flesh and my wife has her own flesh, but we are united as one flesh (plural one.)

This is probably a terrible analogy, but it kind of helped me, in a weird way, to think of 1 x 1 x 1 is still one, what we would call 1^3. (I'm terrible at math, but the calculator says that's right, so I assume it is.)

The point is many Unitarians maintain most Trinitarians (sounds so *West Side Story* here) are actually tritheists, worshipping three separate gods. And a lot of Trinitarians believe many Unitarians don't count Jesus or the Spirit as deity since they only maintain God as One. Both of these arguments are inaccurate. Since I'm not Unitarian, I'll leave it to them to argue how God is One, and Jesus and the Spirit are also God. My point here is not to convert Unitarians, but to define what it means to be Trinitarian, since I believe God is a triune Being, and I'm right. (Smiley face goes here...)

A true Trinitarian only worships one (numerically) God named Yahweh (Jehovah), like the Jews. However, in His singular essence He is represented by three distinct Beings named Father, Son and Holy Spirit. Christians call this the mystery of the Trinity, but in reality, it's not that mysterious. All we're saying is there is one God in essence exhibited in three distinct Persons. I don't find that too hard to swallow. We distinguish the Being of God from the Persons of God, but we don't separate Them: just like we acknowledge the divinity of Jesus as distinct from His humanity, but we don't divide them. (That's coming up in a bit, hang on!)

Just like I am one being, yet I manifest myself in a spirit, soul and body. I cannot separate myself into these three components, but I can perceive they are evident in that I have a physical body anyone can see; a mind, will and emotions no one else can "see" unless I display it to them; and a spirit that communicates with God that no one can "see" but Him.

So now onto these words: *yachiyd* (Strong's #3173, "yah-HEED" where the H sounds like you're clearing your throat) and *echad* (Strong's #259, "eh-HOD," do the same thing with the H) are two Hebrew words that are often translated as some variation of "one."

Yachiyd is used only twelve times in the OT. It means, "one, only, solitary, unique." Oddly enough, it comes from another word *yachad* (Strong's #3161, "yah-HOD," again with the Klingon H) which means "to join or unite"—so "to make one." *Yachiyd* is translated as "only" eight times, referring to an only child. (Ready for this? Genesis 22:2,12,16; Judges 11:34; Proverbs 4:3; Jeremiah 6:26; Amos 8:10; Zechariah 12:10.) Twice it is translated "darling; precious life" in Psalm 22:20 and

35:17—as in, we only have one life to live. Once as "desolate" in Psalm 25:16, and once as "solitary" in Psalm 68:6.

As Strong's definition points out, it can also carry the notion of being "unique." The defense for this is Genesis 22. God calls Isaac Abraham's "only" son, even though Ishmael was also Abraham's son. It's not that God can't count; it's that He is referring to Isaac's uniqueness as being the covenant lineage from whom the Son of God (the only Begotten, "unique") will come—not Ishmael.

A common misconception among Trinitarians is that *yachiyd* cannot refer to God, but this is not true. God is *uniquely* the only God—all other gods are false gods. This is monotheism. It can't be stated clear enough: true Trinitarians are monotheists, not tritheists.

This is the argument many Unitarians put forth, that as Trinitarians, we cannot believe in the *yachiyd* of God. However, we most certainly do believe God is unique; He is indivisibly one God in His existence (state of Being)—in fact, He is the one and only God; there are no others. There is God, and then there is *not* God (everything else.) Reference 1 Corinthians 8:1-6 and Galatians 4:8. He is one God, not three gods.

The difference between the U's and the T's (takes too long to write the words out each time) is the T's believe that One God is manifested in three distinct Persons, made of the same fundamental nature or "quintessence," to use a big word. Therefore, *yachiyd* would refer to the substance of God, but not to His expression.

Rather, this is kind of moot biblically because, in fact, the word *yachiyd* is never used in the Bible as a descriptor for God anyway. One word that *is* used is *echad*. Now note that *echad* is also a derivative of *yachad* (to unite or join.) It is used hundreds of times in the OT—and to be fair to the Oneness group, it does just mean "one." But it has the ability, though *not always*, to define one in an expression of plural unity, as in a herd of sheep is *one* herd of many sheep.

However, we must be careful here, because there is only one God, not many gods. Therefore, it is the context of *echad* that is as important as its definition. We cannot *only* rely on the science of the word without its intent.

This is another of the U's arguments against T's: because *echad* is used in Numbers 13:23, referring to "one cluster of grapes," it therefore cannot define the plurality of the Godhead, since one cluster can be divided into individual grapes; one herd can be split into individual sheep.

But T's do not (or should not, at any rate) apply the *echad* in grapes the same as the *echad* of the Trinity. We maintain the Trinity is indivisible. I cannot separate God the Father from God the Son or God the Spirit. It is all or nothing, three in one, or it is zero. Again, the intent of *echad* is represented in its context.

This brings us to the declaration of Deuteronomy 6:4. The U's point out that if *echad* does not *always* mean plurality of unity, it can also refer to God and still be numerically one. This is true. The T's aren't arguing with you. That's correct: we believe there is only one God.

But in the vast majority of cases *echad* throughout the entirety of the OT shows itself to be collective one.

In the instance of Deuteronomy 6:4, *echad* is attached to "Lord" (*Jehovah, Yahweh*) not "God" (*Elohiym.*) *Elohiym* we've already pointed out is plural singular. So now we're saying *Jehovah* is also plural singular in this context as well.

We have two words here that can be what is termed "uni-plural." *Yahweh* (the Lord) is one united *Elohiym* (God), plural in nature. Of course, this verse doesn't mention the number—we have to use the entirety of scripture to see the Godhead is three.

Look, let's be simple here: *echad*, the word used to describe God in the OT, can mean "one." Numerically. It does not mean "two" or "seventeen." But just like "one" in English, *echad* can mean compounded unity, a group of one, as quite often is the case in the Hebrew.

To say that because *echad* means "one," it unequivocally destroys the concept of Trinity is fuzzy logic—or to be correct, circular reasoning. It uses the hypothesis that God is one... to prove that God is one, when in reality *echad* most certainly can mean one plural.

That's why as a proud T, I emphasize the extreme importance of the oneness of God in light of the threeness of God, and vice versa. Let's not get swept away in tangents, arguing this singular word and ignoring the rest of what God has simply revealed in His Word as Himself being triune—this is why I think the Comma Johanneum is kind of lousy to use as "proof" for U's or T's.

Before we get out of this mind-race, let's point out that the two Greek words used in the NT that correspond to *yachiyd* and *echad* are *heis* (Strong's #1520, "HACE") and *monos* (Strong's #3441, "MON-oss.") Both mean one, *monos* means one and can be plural (Mark 9:2, as just one reference.)

Let me sum up. Understanding the truth of one God represented in three distinct Persons is a significant key to releasing the glory of God in one's life and ministry. The purpose of establishing a balanced doctrine on the Trinity is to keep us equalized between the threeness and oneness of God. If we get off on tangents, placing preeminence on any one of the Persons in the Godhead at the expense of the others, the nature and expression of God becomes clouded and hindered. There is much division and superfluous "doctrine" that comes from attempting to explain the expression of God to His children apart from the biblical revelation of Jehovah. This of course must affect the expression of His glory to the world.

Understanding the personal anointing of God the Son as a Man, understanding the role of the Holy Spirit in working through that anointing power, and understanding the relationship with the Father that is a requirement of that anointing gets convoluted and obscured when placing too much emphasis on the oneness of God.

On the other side of the table, placing too much emphasis on the threeness of God, trying to separate them as individual Gods, or place one expression of the Godhead above the other, destroys the very fabric of what God was intending to demonstrate to His creation in the total unity of the Godhead working in perfect cohesion as one substance expressed in three distinct Persons.

This is not to say that oneness people or extreme Trinitarian people do not see an expression of God's supernatural power released in their lives and ministries. Let us never forget that God is a very gracious God, powerfully merciful, and none of us can fully understand the depth of almighty God.

But these unbalanced theologies lead to hindrances, misconceptions, confusions and in some cases deceptions that stifle the complete flow of God's supernatural might in the day-to-day lives of His people—and out there in the world, where it is so vitally needed.

This is why as truth warriors of the supernatural, we cannot neglect our duties to grasp the concept of a triune, yet singular, God as best as we can.

☷ THE TRUTH OF ☷
THE FATHER

God the Father is the Originator, the Creator, the Masterplanner. It is through Him and by Him—acting in Trinity with the Word and the Spirit—that all of the history of this existence, this universe and our own little slice of it (Earth), came into being. It was He who said to the Word and the Spirit, "Let Us make man in Our image." (Genesis 1:26) And even as those words were said, He knew the plan of salvation that would need to come to pass, the Lamb slain from the foundation of the world (Revelation 13:8), and the Spirit's work in bringing fallen mankind back into communion with Him.

No book on Christian doctrine concerning the glory of the Godhead would be complete without at least a brief study on the Father. And yet, no matter how hard theologians try to outline the attributes of the Creator, humanity falls woefully short in understanding even the smallest portion of God's infinite vastness. It is futile to try and encapsulate a full comprehension of God the Father. I won't even try—let me just give some highlights. My first book, *The Dancing Hand of God*, went to great lengths to study God the Father as best as I could, and even after nearly 175,000 words, I felt pitifully inadequate in describing what nearly four decades in the ministry has revealed about His Personage and expression.

"Oh, the depth of the riches both of the wisdom and knowledge of God! How unsearchable are His judgments and His ways past finding out!" (Romans 11:33)

> "He has made everything beautiful in its time. Also He has put eternity in their hearts, except that no one can find out the work that God does from beginning to end."
>
> (Ecclesiastes 3:11)

The fact of the matter is humanity can have no accurate knowledge of God the Father apart from what He reveals about Himself. When we try with our own faulty reasoning, the best we can come up with is a copy of God, a "graven image" of sorts, and we end up worshiping that which is created instead the One who created. (Romans 1:24)

However, the Father did not want His creation to remain ignorant of Him, and thus revealed some of His nature, character and attributes to mankind through His Word—at least those things that were absolutely required by man to understand in order for him to approach the Father.

Probably one of the greatest "definitions" the Father revealed of Himself was to His friend, Moses:

> "Now the Lord descended in the cloud and stood with him there, and proclaimed the name of the Lord. And the Lord passed before him and proclaimed, 'The Lord, the Lord God, merciful and gracious, longsuffering, and abounding in goodness and truth, keeping mercy for thousands, forgiving iniquity and transgression and sin, by no means clearing the guilty, visiting the iniquity of the fathers upon the children and the children's children to the third and the fourth generation.'"
>
> Exodus 34:5-7

Because God the Father is Truth in every facet of the word and concept, everything that He has revealed about Himself is, therefore, Truth. Such cannot be questioned: if He directly reveals an attribute of Himself in the Word, that attribute is right, correct, truthful, good. (Deuteronomy 32:4; Psalm 119:160; John 17:17)

ATTRIBUTES OF THE FATHER

Let's briefly outline some Truths about the Father. These are not "unknowns," some hidden secret you've never heard before—I'm sure you've figured all these out for yourself, if you've had any kind of experience with God. And yet, sometimes just by expressing these Truths on the printed page, as simple and profound as they are, we firmly profess these attributes of God to be, indeed, Truth. It becomes a part of our spiritual makeup; it sticks with us. And therefore, it's important—especially in a book on Christian doctrine.

So firstly, and I believe very importantly, we must have an understanding of God's holiness. The fact of the matter is there are living creatures that were created for the purpose of declaring His holiness without ceasing. (Revelation 4:8) That's how important His holiness is. Holy means consecrated, set apart, pure, righteous.

What God declares as holy becomes holy, and woe to anything or anyone that would try to defile or profane that holiness. If people had a true revelation of God's utter holiness, they'd quit "messing around" in an instant. We as truth warriors need our own revelation of this utter, awe-full holiness so that we might express that holiness to others.

But we cannot forget that just as God is holy, He is also loving. (1 John 4:8) The Father's heart is turned toward people in love. The kind of love that Paul talks about in 1 Corinthians 13. The world cries out for a revelation of the Father's love. It is up to us as truth warriors to have those kind of "love encounters" with the Father ourselves, so that we may in turn express that love to the lost.

We know that man is not the creator of love, merely the beneficiary of it; we can reciprocate love, but only that love (I mean true love, the kind that sees the miraculous) which we've received from the Father. Our love on its own is not enough.

I've talked elsewhere about focused love (compassion) and developing a sensitivity toward following that divine flow of love—it is a tangible substance that we can perceive through our spiritual senses. At the end of that flow of love, we will find someone to whom the Father wishes to express His love miraculously, be that in a word of knowledge, a gift of healing, whatever the need requires.

Yes, love is caring for our fellow man, doing what we know to be right, helping those who can't help themselves, caring for the poor, the sick, the downtrodden. Indeed we know that, "Pure and undefiled religion before God and the Father is this: to visit orphans and widows in their trouble, and to keep oneself unspotted from the world." (James 1:17)

The Father's heart is for the orphaned—not just physically, but spiritually as well. Those who've been set aside, cast off, looked over. And of course, this is a physical activity—that means, you really do visit orphans and widows in their trouble, for just one chapter later James says:

> "If... one of you says to them, 'Depart in peace, be warmed and filled,' but you do not give them the things which are needed for the body, what does it profit?"
>
> (James 2:16)

But to love someone truly (in Truth) is not only to offer the physical needs, but the spiritual, too. God the Father's love goes beyond taking care of us in a physical sense (though that is important)—but just as much, He meets our spiritual love needs as well. The divine revelation of the Father as Love nourishes every aspect of our lives: spirit, soul and body. It is all miraculous, and all vital. We would do well to cultivate a greater understanding of love.

We tend to gloss over this. "Yeah, love, love, love, I got it. All you need is love. (Someone famous said that once...) Love makes the world go round." But I think it is one of the greatest overlooked attributes of the Father that He wants us to express to others, our fellow Christians and the unloved world at large. I can't say it enough: one of our primary purposes for being a truth warrior of the supernatural is to meet the unmet love needs of a hurting world.

Okay, that almost got sermonizing. I'll behave.

What's next? We know that God is sovereign. Sovereign means independent, self-governing, self-determining, autonomous, ascendant, predominant, superior. It means there is no need for Triune God to ask someone else's permission or opinion on any given matter in the whole of existence.

I don't think anyone who believes in God (the Supreme Being) questions this notion of sovereignty. However, sometimes people seem to take the sovereignty concept in a different angle than I do. Seems that many well-meaning Christians use God's sovereignty as an excuse for what they don't see. "Must not be His will."

I tend to look at it as God's so sovereign He doesn't mind sharing a little bit of that power with His people. He's so sovereign, He doesn't have to be sovereign in every single instance, you know? At least when it comes to us as truth warriors pursuing a supernatural lifestyle. He's not worried about losing His sovereignty if He works with and through His people synergistically.

To be wholly sovereign, as God is, requires He also be entirely self-contained. This word conveys an understanding that the Father requires no outside source to be sustained. There is no "power source" behind God—for He is the power source, completely sufficient in and of Himself, with no other means of support other than Himself. I know this sounds simple, but it really is a truth we must know.

In fact, the Father is so self-supporting, that any other form of existence stems from that abundance of His own source as Himself. Light exists because of Him. Air exists because of Him. Atomic structure exists because of Him.

In other words, all life comes from Him; there is no life that can exist apart from how He wills it. Hmmm. This means there is nothing that anyone can give Him, that He hasn't already given *them* in the first place. Think about that. So we offer our lives to Him, when in reality, they were His to start with. Our worship of Him originated in Him. *Selah.*

> "For as the Father has life in Himself, so He has granted the Son to have life in Himself, and has given Him authority to execute judgment also, because He is the Son of Man."
>
> (John 5:26-27)

We will discuss the three "O's" of Godness in the chapter on Jesus Christ, because it fits in better with the teaching on our Savior's dual nature as fully God and fully Man. But for now, let's highlight the Father's attributes as being omniscient, omnipresent and omnipotent.

Omniscient means having all-knowledge. In fact, we only have knowledge because God has knowledge—it is all "on loan" from Him as a qualification of His all-sufficiency. So, when we say God knows "everything"—that means everything, in all facets, across all of creation, for all eternity, past, present and future.

Nothing will ever surprise God. He is incapable of learning anything new. (That's an interesting thought—something the

Father *can't* do.) Further, He has never "not known" anything before—that's a mind-twister. He has no need to acquire new knowledge, and never had a need to acquire any knowledge in the first place—for it is all His to begin with. His knowledge was/is/will be full and complete. That is what omniscient means.

Same concept in omnipresent. That means "everywhere present." This means that all of creation is contained *within* the Father. The collected "infinite" universe is held by Him. All matter (and anti-matter, if you're into *Star Trek*) is at the same moment immanent and intimate with the Father. Immanent means inherent, intrinsic, innate, ingrained, internalized. A bunch of "I" words, to be homiletic.

Omnipotence means "having all power." Not only owning all power, but being the Source and Originator of all power. It means complete and total authority in every instance. Nothing can happen apart from His yielding or delegating that authority and power to someone else. His influence, control and supremacy is all-inclusive and comprehensive. Nothing happens apart from His permission.

But note, just because His omnipotence is complete, that does not mean His power isn't allotted, assigned or entrusted to others—specifically His creation, mankind, of which is made in His image. He can give out that power to whom He wills. God turned over (or lent out) a portion of His power to Adam, charging him to fill the earth, subdue it, have dominion over the created natural plane. (Genesis 1:28) The Father deputized the man to have power over the world He had created.

This allocated, delegated, designated authority (in a particular sphere of influence, i.e., the earth realm) was forfeited when Adam fell into sin. But even then, God did not rescind that transferred potency—a part of it was pilfered by Satan, and through the work of the cross by the Son, we who are in Him have the means to recover that lost authority.

God the Father is also independently existent. We call this the self-existence of God; it is an attribute that is wholly unique to Him. It resides in the very nature of God and is independent of any other influence or source. If everything else ceased to be, God would still be. He has existed from eternity past, present and future. There was no beginning and there will be no end for God. This is His name, I AM. This is the Latin term *aseity*. It means inherent existence, self-sustaining. He exists because He exists. There can be no other way. This also means He is incapable of ceasing to exist.

This means the Father is eternal. He is timeless, outside the scope of linear thinking concerning a beginning and an end. This does not mean He is incapable of "inserting" Himself into a definite, specific point of space and time—He is immanent and nearby—for He is the creator of space and time. It just means He exists in every aspect and moment of time-space continuously.

It is all present and here to Him. There is no "over there" or "past" or "future." There just IS. And that IS has no break or start or finish. He is infinite in every facet of His existence, without limit, without constraint, without ceasing. This is the eternality of the Father.

And yet, we must also recognize the Father is transcendent, above all else. There is God, and then there is everything else. This has been termed the "Otherness" of God—and I think it's a great title. He is wholly separate and apart from everything else. He is completely Other. He is high and lifted up; there is nothing that is a remotely close second to Him. He surpasses and exceeds *everything* else. It is only because He chooses (or deigns, is probably a better word) to be involved with anything else that He is "near and with us."

God is incapable of changing His nature, His existence, His substance. The make-up of who He is: His essence, His will, His awareness cannot alter or change. There is no ability to vary. This is called immutability, invariability; He is unchangeable.

To be able to change implies an increase or a decrease—a condition of moving to better or worse, a scale of growth or reduction, an ebb and a flow. God cannot change one way or the other, because He is already perfect. There is no fluctuation with the Father.

When we say God is unchanging, it adds a different kind of depth to any other revealed attribute He possesses. If we say He is righteous, virtuous, good, just, blameless, upright and honorable. It means He is incapable of being anything *but* those things—He cannot change.

If we say He is merciful, kindhearted, compassionate, gracious, forbearing and benevolent—it means He is incapable of changing those attributes. If we say God is faithful, believable, truthful, trustworthy, dependable, reliable, constant and loyal— He cannot change. If we say God is wise, prudent, judicious, sagacious, astute—He cannot change.

If we say God is jealous—that cannot change. He will not abide anything but complete devotion, zealousness for His namesake. You're either with Him or not.

It is because of this that God is also a God of wrath. He cannot change this attribute any more than He can change from being a God of love. Wrath is different than emotional anger. It is not an outburst, "Oops, I'm sorry I smote thee, I was wrathful, and lost My temper," said God the Father *never*.

It is a condition of His existence, His holiness. An indignation toward rebellion against Him. Wrath is His morality toward judging sin. It is because He is love that He is wrath. He cannot be perfect with only one attribute without the other. It would then make His demand for a holy life in His people just a trite formality, banal and clichéd—"Do this or I'll give you boils!"

It is because of His love that He demands we follow His commands and chastens His children. (See Proverbs 13:12; Revelation 3:19; Hebrews 12:6.) We cannot have one without the other. If there is no wrath, there is no mercy.

But when we talk about the wrath of God, we must always remember we are not talking about some flippant act of vengeance or retaliation. The intent is not out of malice or cruelty. The wrath of God exists to bring us to the love of God. We would do well not to be so hardhearted and ignorant that we demand that much wrath to get our attention!

We have a choice: to be led by God's eye—"Go this way... "—and that should be enough. Or, we can be led by a bit and a bridle. But we will be led!

> "I will instruct you and teach you in the way you should go; I will guide you with My eye. Do not be like the horse or like the mule, which have no understanding, which must be harnessed with bit and bridle, else they will not come near you."
> (Psalm 32:8-9)

UNVEILING HIS HEART

So, why is it important as truth warriors pressing into the supernatural to have an understanding of the Father's heart? All aspects of creative ministry are rooted not only in our understanding of the Son, the Word, and the Spirit—but also in an unveiling of the Father's heart, the driving desire to reveal the Creator to a world that has a veiled understanding of Him.

It is an apostolic force straight from the Father that releases us into the destinies and purposes the Lord has designed for us—it is by His Son and His Spirit that these destinies are implemented and fulfilled—but the whole concept originates with the Father, the Creative One.

This is why Paul states, "For though you might have ten thousand instructors in Christ, yet you do not have many fathers; for in Christ Jesus I have begotten you through the gospel." (1 Corinthians 4:15)

I believe the body of Christ and the world at large needs a greater understanding of the Father, given through those who have a fathering (mothering) heart. It is the expression of Truth, through the supernatural acts of an apostolic person that ultimately unveil the Father, as best as we can, to those on the earth.

I have said numerous times elsewhere, the glory of God is the Father's reputation being entrusted to us and manifested through us, His sons (and daughters.) Our greatest mandate is to make sure we are representing the Father's glory (reputation) accurately and with integrity. We must, as truth warriors, cultivate an understanding of the Father's nature and grow the kind of character development He requires in order to entrust us with a supernatural expression that unveils His heart to others.

☲ THE TRUTH OF ☲ GOD'S NAMES

Following the doctrine of Trinity and the Father, let's insert a short study on the truth that God revealed of Himself in His Word. This is theology in its simplest terms, and we have highlighted elements of God's nature in the previous chapters, but let's look at specifically what God says about Himself in His Word. Specifically, I want to compile a fairly exhaustive (I might have missed a couple here and there) list for the names of God.

Why is this important? I'm glad you asked. Nowadays our names are just that... names. Some don't even have meanings and we just make them up. But biblically, names matter. They not only identify a person, they are often a reflection of the person's character or worth. Their reputation is carried in the name. Ever wondered why so often a person in the Bible's name ends up *meaning* what they did or how they were? Like Nabal in 1 Samuel 25, his name literally means "fool." Odd how it worked out like that.

But in the past, names were often important as descriptors of the person to whom they were attached. To a certain extent that is true today, but the importance of one's name in modern times pales in comparison to names from the time of the Bible.

The names of God are no different. They are not simply labels but actually reveal an expression of His character and worth, His reputation being manifested. For you wonderful people who've read *Dancing Hand*, you'll recall *doxa* (Strong's #1391, something like "DOAX-uh") is translated "glory" and means "a good opinion of something's worth." God's glory is His reputation being put to the test. These names He reveals in the Word are the titles representing that worth. Therefore, as truth warriors of the supernatural, it's important we know these names, right?

Indeed, we are saved in Jesus' name according to John 1:12 and Acts 4:12. And of course, we understand it is not some mystical formula in the name of Jesus Himself, but rather belief in what that name represents—the power, the authority, the glory behind that name.

"I am the Lord, that is My name; and My glory I will not give to another, nor My praise to carved images." (Isaiah 42:8)

> "Then men began to call on the name of the Lord... There he built an altar to the Lord and called on the name of the Lord... So he built an altar there and called on the name of the Lord..."
> (Genesis 4:26, 12:8, 26:25)

These verses (there are many others) show us that calling upon the name of the Lord is an act of worship to Him. Conversely, it was an act of blasphemy not to hold the name of the Lord sacred—the Levitical instructions were clear the Lord's name was not to be profaned by treating the offerings given to Him disrespectfully. (Leviticus 22) And we all know (or should know!) the Third Commandment given in Exodus 20:7 and Deuteronomy 5:11.

Observant Jews today do not utter the name of God aloud (although some do write it) and often use the word "*HaShem*" ("the Name") when referring to Him in day-to-day life or will use the word *Adonai* ("my Lords") when praying. (Interestingly, *Adonai* is plural, but of course I've commented enough on this in the Trinity chapter—you'll have to make up your own mind.)

Some Jews (and even a few Christians) are so concerned about taking the Name lightly, they spell it G-d in English, just to be sure. (Some throw the pen away after writing the Name, and many believe it is sin to erase the Name.)

Now, the Bible makes no such prohibition, and biblical evidence supports that people in the Old Testament did pronounce His name aloud; we are just warned that the Name is not to be used capriciously. I'm not going to harp on some Christians who follow modern Judaic tradition, but for myself, I have no problem reverently using His name aloud.

YHWH

> "Then Moses said to God, 'Indeed, when I come to the children of Israel and say to them, "The God of your fathers has sent me to you," and they say to me, "What is His name?" what shall I say to them?' And God said to Moses, 'I AM WHO I AM.' And He said, 'Thus you shall say to the children of Israel, "I AM has sent me to you."' Moreover God said to Moses, 'Thus you shall say to the children of Israel: "The Lord God of your fathers, the God of Abraham, the God of Isaac, and the God of Jacob, has sent me to you. This is My name forever, and this is My memorial to all generations."'
> (Exodus 3:13-15)

In the above passage, there are actually three names for God: I AM THAT I AM, I AM (a contraction of the longer name) and finally God (YHWH, *Yahweh*.) I AM THAT I AM in Hebrew is *Ehyeh Asher Ehyeh*: quite literally, "I shall be that I shall be." It has been widely discredited that it means, "I shall be *what* I shall be" which implies a sense of ambiguousness. So technically, His name is His state of eternal existence. "I AM" or "He is (always.)" Because really, when He just IS—what name could possibly be given for Him that we could understand? Yet, in spite of our dimmed comprehension of what it means to be "is," God reveals a lot about Himself with His names. First, notice the similarity between *Ehyeh* and *Yahweh*.

Ancient Hebrew was written without vowels. So the name of God was put down as YHWH (*Yahweh*), and because of this, no one is 100% sure how the word is supposed to be pronounced.

(Certain Kabbalah sects claim to know how it is pronounced, as do some pseudo-Christian cults stemming from groups like Knights Templar and Freemasonry.)

These four letters are called the Tetragrammaton (a foolishly long transliterated Greek word that means "a word with four letters." Isn't that deep? The word describing the four letters is much longer than just the four letters! Go figure.)

YHWH appears nearly 7,000 times in the Hebraic Bible. It's first appearance is Genesis 2:4, and in most cases it's written as LORD, with a capital L and small capitals ord. In English, we often transliterate the word into JHVH, which we pronounce Jehovah. The word specifically "god"—which we discussed before as *El*—is coupled with YHWH to make "Lord God." (Most times *El* is not used in the Bible alone, since it just means "god," especially concerning the Lord, but is mostly compounded with another word to ensure that everyone knows the writer means the Hebrew God, YHWH.)

Back in the Dark Ages, God was sometimes called "The Seven," in reference to His seven holy names. We've discussed most of these names already: Elohim (and the singular Eloah), Yahweh, I AM, and Adonai. The other two are *El Shaddai*, meaning the Almighty God (the God of more than enough, the most ample God)—which for you fine readers of *Dancing Hand*, you'll recall that more than likely Shaddai carries a concept of having surplus milk for one's children. The last (numerically not positionally) is often connected to YHWH, as in *Yahweh Tzevat* (*Jehovah-Sabaoth*), meaning "The Lord of Hosts." He is God over the armies (of Israel and the heavenly host.) (For references, see Exodus 6, 7; 1 Samuel 17:45; and Psalm 46:7.)

Not only does He control the awesome power of the hosts of heaven, but He is the chief Warrior for His children, fighting their battles for them, infinitely strong and full of valor. His strength is untold; the might of His arm is limitless. Enemies tremble at the mere mention of His name. How's that for a revelation of truth in His supernatural power? Praise the Lord of Hosts!

REDEMPTIVE NAMES

Jehovah-Sabaoth is sometimes listed with the seven redemptive names of Jehovah. These are widely known in Christian circles, yet a chapter on the names of God wouldn't be complete without including them. Further, each of these important names reveals an attribute, a characteristic of the God we serve. Each name has an extremely essential unveiling aspect of God's supernatural power. Again, these names are not formulaic—they're not some secret codeword we whisper to "get" God to move. They are a revelation of His very existence. They are not things He can do—they are things that He IS. These redemptive names are a by-product of His very existence.

These seven names are often called covenant names of the Lord; they are promises the Lord has made to His children, those who follow His commandments and make Him Lord of their lives.

> "Then Abraham lifted his eyes and looked, and there behind him was a ram caught in a thicket by its horns. So Abraham went and took the ram, and offered it up for a burnt offering instead of his son. And Abraham called the name of the place, The-Lord-Will-Provide; as it is said to this day, 'In the Mount of the Lord it shall be provided.'"
> (Genesis 22:13-14)

The first (in the Bible, not in preeminence, for they are all equal names) is *Jehovah-Jireh*: "the Lord will provide." Remember that chorus from way back when: "Jehovah Jireh, my provider, His strength is sufficient for me, for me, for me!"

I suppose precisely, in old English, J's are pronounced Y's, so it's "Yehovah Yireh" (yeer-ay.) *Yir'eh* actually means the Lord "sees," as in He understands and perceives our needs, and thus meets them.

> "If you diligently heed the voice of the Lord your God and do what is right in His sight, give ear to His commandments and keep all His statutes, I will put none of the diseases on you which I have brought on the Egyptians. For I am the Lord who heals you."
> (Exodus 15:26)

Next in the Bible is *Jehovah-Rapha*: "the Lord who heals you." The name Raphael means "God has healed." Rapha is a dynamic revelation of the restorative/preservation power of God. Notice it is in the context of a covenantal promise, "if you will... then I will." The covenantal names have conditional attachments, a response is required by mankind.

The Rapha name of God is one of the most powerful in regards to us as truth warriors bringing forth a supernatural manifestation of His might and grace; the vast majority of people out there need some kind of healing, physically, emotionally or spiritually. Again, for you wonderful *Dancing Hand* readers, you might recall the concept is of a physician mending a wound by stitching. Jehovah-Rapha also refers to spiritual and emotional healing. Complete restoration and preservation for those who are in a covenant relationship with Jehovah. I know of no other religion in the world that offers a similar "deal."

"And Moses built an altar and called its name, The-Lord-Is-My-Banner..." (Exodus 17:15)

This name is *Jehovah-Nissi*, and the revelation of this covenant name comes from Moses' response to the Lord's victory over the Amalekites, whom the Lord proclaimed He would utterly blot out their remembrance from under the face of heaven. It is generally considered correct that the Amalekites were descendants of Amalek, the grandson of Esau, and there's some speculation that the Amalekites might have been very tall, since the Arab word for "giant" is quite similar.

Whether or not this is the absolute truth, it conveys an interesting parallel of God's complete triumph over carnality (the profane spirit of Esau.) A banner is a military standard, a war flag, that troops rally around. It is where we get the phrase, "set the standard" or being "held to a higher standard." This covenant name reveals that God is our banner of victory—that the battle belongs to Him wholly, and the victory we share is from rallying around that Standard, God Himself.

"So Gideon built an altar there to the Lord, and called it The-Lord-Is-Peace. To this day it is still in Ophrah of the Abiezrites." (Judges 6:24)

This compound name is *Jehovah-Shalom*. Isaiah 9:6 describes the Lord Jesus as the Prince of Peace. One of the main focuses in the plan of salvation was the restoration of peace between God and man. The Psalms share many references to the peace of God. A quick search yielded the following scriptures: Psalm 29:11, 32:17, 34:14, 37:37, 85:8 and 119:165—that's probably not exhaustive.

One of the hallmarks of the Lord's ministry on earth was peace. He is called the God of love and peace and the Lord of peace. (2 Corinthians 13:11; 2 Thessalonians 3:16) According to Romans 14, the kingdom of God is righteous, joy and peace in the Holy Spirit. Malachi 2:5 speaks of a covenant of life and peace. As truth warriors of the supernatural, our revelation of God's peace and how it is translated to others—the peace that surpasses all understanding (Philippians 4:7)—is an effective blessing of truth that sets one free.

The concept of *shalom* is not just peace in the strictest sense of the word: the opposite of hostilities; amity and harmony between two people, two nations, God and man, etc. It also means "wholeness or completeness," a state of well-being, of faring well. Stillness, calmness, quiet, tranquility, serenity. All of these describe the *shalom* of God. Jehovah-Shalom does not promise that life is a bed of roses with no difficulties, setbacks, ups-and-downs; but He promises that the attribute of His very nature (peace) can be the portion for those who follow Him. We can live in completeness and wholeness even in the midst of trials, tribulations, difficulties, dearth and drama, when the Lord is Lord of our lives. Every Christian should study Psalm 46 until they have it memorized. (I'm not there yet, but I'm still studying!)

"The Lord is my shepherd; I shall not want." (Psalm 23:1)

Even though the word "is" separates it, that's actually the compound name *Jehovah-Ra-ah* (some have it as *Roi* or *Rohi*.) *Ra-ah* would be pronounced "raw-aw" or something similar to that.

That God Almighty would condescend to the concept of being a simple shepherd watching over a flock is staggering, because let's be honest, shepherds aren't really considered powerful people in this world, you know? And then to attach Shepherd to His *name* (His glory and reputation) creates an even greater astonishment. It's not just a concept anymore, it's part of who He is. A Shepherd. And yes, a Warrior, and yes, a mighty King. But He's also a meek Shepherd, seeking the peace and well-being of the flock.

Now, before we get too puffed up, who is the Lord the Shepherd of? His people, you and me. So… that makes us sheep. And sheep aren't too smart, if you've ever spent any time in the presence of one. But, you say, lambs are cute, right? Sure. But smart? Meh, not so much… There's a *reason* sheep need a shepherd, you know? Left on their own, they'd find ways to get themselves killed. (Ever read *Heidi* as a kid growing up?) Just not a whole lot going on upstairs in a sheep's mind.

So while the Lord may condescend to calling Himself a Shepherd, He also requires us to call ourselves His sheep. And I'm okay with that, 'cause I've done some things in my life that were about as intelligent as a sheep, and it was only by the Shepherd's guidance, mercy and grace, I didn't stumble over a cliff to my death. I'm sure you can think of a few instances in your life that were pretty similar. So say it with me, Baa-baa!

Psalm 23 is arguably the most famous of Bible passages, at least probably the most well-known of the Psalms. I mean, just about every Christian out there can quote it. The concept of the Lord leading His flock beside calm, peaceful waters, comforting us with His rod and staff, anointing our heads with oil—to know that this not just something He does, but something He IS… wow, that's a revelation.

"In His days Judah will be saved, and Israel will dwell safely; now this is His name by which He will be called: THE LORD OUR RIGHTEOUSNESS." (Jeremiah 23:6)

Next, in left to right order in the Bible, we find *Jehovah-Tsidkenu*. The context of this revelation (the Lord Our Righteousness) is interesting to note: here's stubborn, rebellious, idolatrous Israel, heading to exile and slavery—and the Lord is promising, in the fullness of days, He Himself would become their righteousness, through the Son. It is a future proclamation, a prophetic decree, that wouldn't find its fulfillment for, what, like six centuries.

And yet, here we are, millennia later, able to call ourselves in right-standing, blameless, before the Righteous One, because of His Son's sacrifice on the cross. It's an amazing decree of hope to an otherwise hopeless group of people. When we declare the righteousness of God, we display our own righteousness—solely through the shed blood of Jesus Christ—to the world at large. Humbling, and comforting, in the same thought.

As truth warriors of the supernatural, we need to have an understanding of our place before the Lord, for our ability to make a demand on the supernatural anointing, stems from the Lord, thousands of years prior, declaring that in "that day"—the day of the Lord's death, resurrection, ascension—His righteous becomes our righteousness, and everything He stands for, everything that goes into His name, becomes our portion. Praise God!

"All the way around shall be eighteen thousand cubits; and the name of the city from that day shall be: THE LORD IS THERE." (Ezekiel 48:35)

The prophet Ezekiel has a vision of the restoration of the City of Jerusalem, metaphorically, the restoration of the people of God.

Not only a physical occurrence, but rather, a future, spiritual occurrence found in the Church of the Lord Jesus Christ—you and me and our fellow brethren in the Lord. It is comforting to know that the Lord is *here* with us, present. Not only just a dim understanding of a future eternity spent with Him being THERE. But He is HERE now, for we are the Lord's city.

And yes, the same city in John's Revelation is this city Ezekiel saw (twelve gates, the 4,500 cubits to a side, etc.) So God will *always* be THERE, residing with His people. How awesome!

"O Lord, our Lord, how excellent is Your name in all the earth, who have set Your glory above the heavens!" (Psalm 8:1)

THAT'S A LOT OF NAMES

"I will worship toward Your holy temple, and praise Your name for Your lovingkindness and Your truth; for You have magnified Your word above all Your name." (Psalm 138:2)

Remember those posters in a rainbow of colors that listed just tons and tons of titles for God? I always liked those. So I wanted to provide a similar list. Not all of these are names for God in the strictest sense; many are attributes and titles of His Personage. But since we know that His Name, magnified second only to His Word, is more of a declaration of His character and reputation (His glory manifested) than just simply titles, I think it's important to know what the Bible has at one time or another called the Lord God. At the very least, it'll bless you to read them. Take a moment, meditate on them. Think about what each one is saying concerning the supernatural unction, the reputation of God, resting upon you as a truth warrior. I might suggest underlining them in your Bible—takes some time, but it's worthwhile!

I'm sure I missed some—it's a big Bible, after all. But this is a whole lot of 'em!

Now, keep in mind, the sum-total of each of these attributes is found in the Lord Jesus, God Himself, our great King, Friend, High Priest, Example and Enabler. So when we move into the next chapter on the Messiah, keep as many of these titles in your mind as you can.

OLD TESTAMENT

Genesis
Angel of the Lord (16:7)
Breath of Life (2:7)
Everlasting God (21:33)
Exceedingly Great Reward (15:1)
God (1:1)
God Almighty (17:1)
God Most High (14:20)
God who Sees (16:13)
Lord Will Provide (22:14)
Seed of the Woman (3:15)
Shield (15:1)
Shiloh (49:10)
Spirit of God (1:2)
Stone of Israel (49:24)

Exodus
I AM (3:14)
Jealous (34:14)
Lord (4:10)
Lord Is My Banner (17:15)
Lord who Heals You (15:26)
Lord who Sanctifies You (31:13)
Man of War (15:3)
My Song (15:2)

Leviticus
Lord who Sanctifies You (20:8)

Numbers
Glory of the Lord (14:21)
Scepter (24:17)
Star out of Jacob (24:17)

Deuteronomy
As an Eagle (32:11)
Eternal God (33:27)
Rock (32:4)
Shield of Your Help (33:29)
Sword of Your Majesty (33:29)

Judges
Lord Is Peace (6:24)

2 Samuel
Rock of My Salvation (22:47)
Shield/Buckler (22:31)

1 Kings
Still Small Voice (19:12)

Job

Redeemer (19:25)

Psalms

Anointed One (2:2)
Creator (40:28)
Defender of Widows (68:5)
Deliverer (144:2)
Dwelling Place/Refuge (90:1)
Everlasting God (40:28)
Exalted/Excellent (148:13)
Father of the Fatherless (68:5)
Fortress (144:2)
Guide (48:14)
Hiding Place (32:7)
High Tower (144:2)
Jehovah (83:18)
Keeper (121:5)
King of Glory (24:10)
Lord My Shepherd (23:1)
Lovingkindness (144:2)
Maker (95:6)
Most High (91:1)
My King, O God (44:4)
My Light (27:1)
My Portion (73:26)
Refuge (144:2)
Shade at Your Right Hand (121:5)
Shield (144:2)
The One (144:2)
Yah (68:4)
Yahweh (83:18)

Proverbs

Strong Tower (18:10)

Song of Solomon

Lily of the Valleys (2:1)
Rose of Sharon (2:1)

Isaiah

Arm of the Lord (53:1)
Child (9:6)
Crown of Beauty (28:5)

Diadem of Beauty (28:5)
Elect One (42:1)
Everlasting Father (9:6)
Glory of God (60:1)
God of the Whole Earth (54:5)
Holy One of Israel (41:14)
Husband (54:5)
Immanuel (7:14)
Judge (33:22)
King (33:22)
Lawgiver (33:22)
Light to the Gentiles (42:6)
Lord of Hosts (6:3)
Man of Sorrows (53:3)
Mighty God (9:6)
Mighty One of Jacob (60:16)
Most Upright (26:7)
Our Potter (64:8)
Place of Broad Rivers and Streams (33:21)
Prince of Peace (9:6)
Redeemer (41:14)
Refuge from the Storm (25:4)
Rock of Offense (8:14)
Sanctuary (8:14)
Servant (42:1)
Shadow from the Heat (25:4)
Spirit of Counsel and Might (11:2)
Spirit of Knowledge and of the Fear of the Lord (11:2)
Spirit of Wisdom and Understanding (11:2)
Strength to the Needy (25:4)
Stone (28:16)
Stone of Stumbling (8:14)
Wonderful Counselor (9:6)

Jeremiah

Branch of Righteousness (33:15)
Fountain of Living Waters (2:13)
He Shall Recompense (51:6)
Lord Our Righteousness (23:6)
Merciful (3:12)
Mighty, Awesome One (20:11)
My Fortress (16:19)

My Refuge (16:19)
My Strength (16:19)

Ezekiel
Lord is There (48:35)

Daniel
Ancient of Days (7:9)
Living God (6:20)

Micah
Ruler in Israel (5:2)

Nahum
Good (1:7)
Stronghold (1:7)

Haggai
Desire of All Nations (2:7)

Zechariah
My Servant the Branch (3:8)
Fountain (13:1)
Wall of Fire (2:5)
Your King (9:9)

Malachi
Launderer's Soap (3:2)
Messenger of the Covenant (3:1)
Purifier of Silver (3:3)
Refiner (3:3)
Refiner's Fire (3:2)
Sun of Righteousness (4:2)

NEW TESTAMENT

Matthew
Bridegroom (9:15)
Christ (1:16)
Emmanuel (1:23)
Father (6:9)
Friend of Sinners (11:19)
God with Us (1:23)
Governor (2:6)
Jesus (1:21)
King of Israel (27:42)
King of the Jews (27:11)
Lord of the Harvest (9:38)
Master (23:8)
Nazarene (2:23)
Son of Abraham (1:1)
Son of David (1:1; 15:22)
Son of God (27:54)
Son of Man (18:11)
Son of the Living God (16:16)
Teacher (26:18)

Mark
Carpenter (6:3)
Son of Mary (6:3)

Luke
Anointed (4:18)
Bridegroom (5:35)
Christ of God (9:20)
Christ the Lord (2:11)
Consolation of Israel (2:25)
Dayspring (1:78)
God My Savior (1:47)
Highest (1:76)
Horn of Salvation (1:69)
Master (5:5)
Physician (4:23)
Son of God (1:35)
Son of the Most High (1:32)

John
Bread of God (6:33)
Bread of Life (6:35)

Comforter (14:26)
Door of the Sheep (10:7)
Friend (15:15)
Gift of God (4:10)
Good Shepherd (10:11)
Helper (15:26)
Holy Spirit (14:26)
I AM (8:58)
King of Israel (1:49)
Lamb of God (1:29)
Life (11:25; 14:6)
Light of the World (8:12)
Living Water (4:10)
Lord (13:13)
Messiah (1:41; 4:25)
My Lord and My God (20:28)
Only Begotten Son (1:18)
Rabbi (1:49)
Resurrection (11:25)
Spirit (4:24)
Spirit of Truth (15:26)
Teacher (20:16)
True Light (1:9)
True Vine (15:1)
Truth (14:6)
Way (14:6)
Word (1:1)
Vine (15:5)
Vinedresser (15:1)

Acts
God of Abraham, Isaac and Jacob (3:13)
Holy One (2:27)
Just One (22:14)
Lord of All (10:36)
Prince of Life (3:15)
Promise of the Father (1:4)
Prophet (3:22)

Romans
Abba (8:15)
Deliverer (11:26)
Firstborn (8:29)

Godhead (1:20)
Intercessor (8:26)
Jesus Christ Our Lord (6:23)
Over All (9:5)
Spirit of Adoption (8:15)

1 Corinthians
Author of Peace (14:33)
Christ the Power of God (1:24)
Christ the Wisdom of God (1:24)
Firstfruits (15:23)
Foundation (3:11)
Last Adam (15:45)
Life-giving Spirit (15:45)
Lord Jesus Christ (15:57)
Lord of Glory (2:8)
Our Passover (5:7)
Rock (10:4)

2 Corinthians
Image of God (4:4)
Spirit (3:17)

Galatians
Seed of Abraham (3:16)

Ephesians
Chief Cornerstone (2:20)
Head of the Church (5:23)
Our Peace (2:14)
Sacrifice (5:2)
Savior of the Body (5:23)

Colossians
All and in All (3:11)
Firstborn from the Dead (1:18)
Head of the Body/Church (1:18)

1 Thessalonians
Avenger (4:6)
Living and True God (1:9)

1 Timothy
King Eternal (1:17)
Mediator (2:5)
Potentate (6:15)
Ransom (2:6)

2 Timothy
Seed of David (2:8)

Titus
Blessed Hope (2:13)
Glorious Appearing (2:13)

Hebrews
Apostle (3:1)
Author of Eternal Salvation (5:9)
Author/Finisher of our Faith (12:2)
Brightness of His Glory Heb1:3
Captain of Their Salvation (2:10)
Consuming Fire (12:29)
Eternal Spirit (9:14)
Express Image of His Person (1:3)
Great High Priest (4:14)
Great Shepherd (13:20)
Heir of All Things (1:2)
High Priest (3:1)
High Priest Forever (6:20)
Majesty on High (1:3)
Priest (4:15)
Rewarder (11:6)

James
Father of Lights (1:17)

1 Peter
Creator (4:19)
Overseer of Souls (2:25)
Chief Shepherd (5:4)
Living Stone (2:4)
Shepherd (2:25)
Stone (2:8)

2 Peter
Day Star (1:19)

1 John
Advocate (2:1)
Eternal Life (5:27)
Love (4:8)
Propitiation (2:2)
Jesus Christ the Righteous (2:1)

Revelation
Alpha and Omega (21:6)
Amen (3:14)
Beginning and End (21:6)
Bright and Morning Star (22:16)
Faithful and True (19:11)
Faithful and True Witness (3:14)
King of Kings (19:16)
King of Saints (15:3)
Lord God Almighty (15:3)
Lord of Lords (19:16)
Lion of the Tribe of Judah (5:5)
Root/Offspring of David (22:16)
Ruler of God's Creation (3:14)
Ruler over Kings of Earth (1:5)
Temple (21:22)
Word of God (19:13)

☰ THE TRUTH OF ☰
JESUS CHRIST

Perfect. We're going to be studying this word in its fullest capacity. Perfection incarnate. The most perfect. This is going to be the best chapter in the book, in my humblest of opinions, because it's going to talk about my favorite Person. The past few chapters have been heavily laden with technical teaching, and rightfully so. I want to thank you for giving them their proper time in studying, so as a reward, let's spend several pages enjoying the perfectness of our Lord, Jesus Christ.

Christianity is attacked all over the world, and the greatest ammunition that assailants bring forth is contesting just who Jesus was. God? A man? Historical fact places the birth of the Man named Jesus in the town of Bethlehem around 7-2 BC, with the general consensus narrowing it down between 6-4 BC, during the reign of Herod the Great and the Roman census of Judea. Many scientists, including Sir Isaac Newton, placed the date of His death to be Friday, April 23, 34 AD—while some say Friday, April 3, 33 AD. However, no one denies the existence of a Jew named Jesus who was killed by Roman crucifixion.

Interestingly enough for a book on "truth," one of the most dramatic scenes in history has to be Jesus standing before Pontius Pilate, who utters a question that's plagued philosophers for centuries: "What is truth?" (John 18:38) As these words leave Pilate's lips, who's the first to hear them? The Man who just hours earlier declared Himself the Way, the Truth and the Life. (John 14:6) How tragically sad that someone as powerful, educated, as Pilate could look Truth in the eye and not recognize it! But as Paul said, people are "always learning and never able to come to the knowledge of the truth." (2 Timothy 3:7)

Knowledge for many people is god, because they innately know that learning truth solves problems; but knowledge acquired apart from the Truth can lead to deeper darkness and confusion. This is not to say that earthly knowledge, in and of itself, is evil or of no worth—let us always grow in knowledge, but let us be wary of its pitfalls. We as born-again believers have a tremendous advantage over the rest of the world's truth-seekers, because we know that the truth is in the Christ and His Word.

He as Truth incarnate identified with truth in scripture when He prayed to His Father, on behalf of His own, saying, "Sanctify them by Your truth. Your word is truth." (John 17:17)

Let's look at some truths about the Truth. Who was this Man? Was He God? Was He man? Actually, He was both.

There are tons of contentious beliefs even among Christianity concerning who Christ was. Some deny His deity. Some deny His humanity. Some deny two natures within Christ; some say two natures were blended into a third; some say He was a man filled with God, or God filled with man.

So in 451 AD, a church council was held in Chalcedon to address these controversies, and out of that comes the

Chalcedonian Creed, which is as follows (please read it, even though it's VERY detailed!):

"We, then, following the holy Fathers, all with one consent, teach people to confess one and the same Son, our Lord Jesus Christ, the same perfect in Godhead and also perfect in manhood; truly God and truly man, of a reasonable [this means, "rational"] soul and body; consubstantial [this means, "co-essential, of the same substance as"] with the Father according to the Godhead, and consubstantial with us according to the Manhood; in all things like unto us, without [or "except"] sin; begotten before all ages of the Father according to the Godhead, and in these latter days, for us and for our salvation, born of the Virgin Mary, the Mother of God, according to the Manhood; one and the same Christ, Son, Lord, only begotten, to be acknowledged in two natures, inconfusedly, unchangeably, indivisibly, inseparably; [in the Greek and Latin: ἐν δύο φύσεσιν ἀσυγχύτως, ἀτρέπτως, ἀδιαιρέτως, ἀχωρίστως—*in duabus naturis inconfuse, immutabiliter, indivise, inseparabiliter,* meaning in English, "without confusion, without conversion, indivisible and inseparable"]; the distinction of natures being by no means taken away [or "abolished"] by the union, but rather the property of each nature being preserved, and concurring in one Person ["*prosopon,*" the self-manifestation, or "person, face, countenance"] and one Subsistence [what we call, "*hypostasis,*" or the "Hypostatic Union" of the Christ's two natures], not parted or divided into two persons, but one and the same Son, and μονογενῆ Θεὸν [in English, "only begotten God"], the Word, the Lord Jesus Christ; as the prophets from the beginning [have declared] concerning Him, and the Lord Jesus Christ Himself has taught us, and the Creed of the holy Fathers has handed down to us."

Whew, I need a drink of water after saying all that! I mean, wow, how's that for technical! And here I was telling you this chapter was gonna be easier than the previous! Now, memorize that whole thing in five minutes 'cause you're being tested later.

Hey, let's sum this up real simply without all the Greek and Latin. The bottom line is this: truth-seekers like you and me believe Jesus Christ was fully God, and fully Man, not half-and-half. That there were TWO natures in one Person, a divine nature and a human nature, discernible but undividable, united so that no third "hybrid" nature was formed. See, perfect. In all facets.

Okay, why is this important? Only one Person, both completely God and completely Man, could stand as a Mediator between the Father and mankind, redeeming the latter from judgment because of sin against God.

"For there is one God and one Mediator between God and men, the Man Christ Jesus…" (1 Timothy 2:5)

GOD IN THE FLESH

Let's look at His dual natures. But first, let's establish His divinity in the flesh. Jesus was always and will always be God—divine, sinless, holy, righteous, good, wise. Perfect. He was/is/will always be the Word, and we've already discussed this from John 1:1. He is coequal with the Father and the Holy Spirit, represented in the Trinity.

The Bible, which we've already established as the supreme, ultimate, uncontestable authority on Christian doctrine (the truth), makes it very clear the Messiah is God (and that Jesus is the Messiah.)

> "Therefore the Lord Himself will give you a sign: behold, the virgin shall conceive and bear a Son, and shall call His name Immanuel... For unto us a Child is born, unto us a Son is given; and the government will be upon His shoulder. And His name will be called Wonderful, Counselor, Mighty God, Everlasting Father, Prince of Peace."
>
> (Isaiah 7:14, 9:6)

Immanuel literally means "God-with-us." It is interesting to point out that the Messiah is also called Everlasting Father.

The Savior, the coming Messiah, is called LORD (the name of God, Jehovah) in the Old Testament. I bet you want those scriptures, huh? Okay. Hosea 1:7 and Isaiah 12:2.

The Messiah actually speaks of Himself in the Old Testament:

> "And I will pour on the house of David and on the inhabitants of Jerusalem the Spirit of grace and supplication; then they will look on Me whom they pierced. Yes, they will mourn for Him as one mourns for his only son, and grieve for Him as one grieves for a firstborn."
>
> (Zechariah 12:10)

"I will declare the decree: the Lord has said to Me, 'You are My Son, today I have begotten You.'" (Psalm 2:7)

Thus, the Word took on human flesh (this is called the "Incarnation") and was born on this earth from a virgin mother, begotten by God the Father. It is not man becoming God, but God became man as Jesus. Though the Father begot Him, He was born of a virgin woman, so the Messiah, Jesus, was also a Man and not some kind of demigod, half-and-half creature. Genesis 3:15 is the first mention of this coming Messiah, directly after the fall of mankind. Remember the previous chapter that pointed out the first mentioning of something in the Bible is important. This is why! It clearly shows that God would be born from the seed of woman—entirely human, yet entirely God.

The Bible also makes several mentions of Christ's complete humanity, coming from the seed of Abraham—the nation of Israel, specifically of the tribe of Judah, the house of David. This makes Him humanly the lawful King of the Jews. I bet you want those scripture verses, don't you? Okay. Highlight these real quick: Genesis 49:10; Numbers 24:17,19; 2 Samuel 7:12-14; Isaiah 11:1-2. Thank me later, we're moving quickly here.

Why did Jesus have to be fully human? Because God could not compensate for man's sin as God; only man could die in the stead of man. Animal sacrifices were not enough for complete restitution; they were a type, a foreshadowing. Sin must be punished by death. (Romans 6:23 and 5:12-21) Yet God, who must be sinless, could not offer Himself as God, because that would mean coming under sin, and He wouldn't, then, be God.

Yet only a sinless being (God) could fully redeem the sinful with His death. So what must He do? God would have to become Man (clothe Himself in flesh), yet still remain God.

So why did Jesus have to come from the Father in heaven? Because He would have to be completely free of sin; otherwise, He would not be an acceptable (complete, perfect) sacrifice for sin.

Only two men were ever in this world that were originally free from sin: Adam and Jesus. Adam would've been immortal, living forever, with a perfect nature, corrupted in no way, with no sickness, no death.

But when Adam fell, now knowing the difference between good and evil, he inherited a sin nature, which is death. Spiritually, Adam died the moment the fruit of the Tree of the Knowledge of Good and Evil touched his lips because the Lord told him:

> "Of every tree of the garden you may freely eat; but of the tree of the knowledge of good and evil you shall not eat, for **in the day** that you eat of it you shall surely die."
> (Genesis 2:16-17, emphasis added)

Now Adam physically died over 900 years later, but his spirit became deadened to God the moment he ate the fruit.

It's interesting to note that God never commanded Adam not to eat of the Tree of Life, which was also in the garden of Eden. (Genesis 2:9) Had he eaten of that fruit, we wouldn't be in the mess we are in now.

See, because of Original Sin (we'll also get into that later— little teasers to keep you reading!) the sin nature is passed down through the seed of man, from Adam all the way down to you and me. Every human being is born with a sin nature; we all must be redeemed. So if God had just "inhabited" a human body of both human parents, it would have contained a sin nature—already corrupted from its first breath.

"Therefore, just as through one man sin entered the world, and death through sin, and thus death spread to all men, because all sinned..." (Romans 5:12)

However, Jesus is the second Adam, the last Adam.

> "For as in Adam all die, even so in Christ all shall be made alive... And so it is written, 'The first man Adam became a living being.' The last Adam became a life-giving spirit."
>
> (1 Corinthians 15:22,45)

The only way to be completely sin-free would have to be born not of man, but of God, since God is devoid of sin. However, to be completely man, one must be born of a human. How is this accomplished? Through the miracle of the Incarnation. The Holy Spirit, who is God as well, overshadowed Mary, a virgin, and she conceived a Child.

> "And the angel answered and said to her, 'The Holy Spirit will come upon you, and the power of the Highest will overshadow you; therefore, also, that Holy One who is to be born will be called the Son of God.'"
>
> (Luke 1:35)

One of the key elements of Christianity is the virgin birth—a miracle—because it means that God was born into mankind.

Deity took on humanity (not the other way round.) Some people try to downplay this, claiming that Jesus never said He was deity. Kinda foolish, really; see Matthew 22:42-46. Or what about most of John, Chapter 6, like verses 33 to 62! Or John, Chapter 8, like verses 23-25 and 56-58 (that's so explicitly I AM!) In fact, nearly all of the Book of John's "I am" quotes by Jesus, He uses "I AM" (the name for God)—that's why they wanted to kill Him, for blasphemy! And then there's John 17:23-25 and Revelation 1:8. I hope you're marking all these down in your Bible—you don't want to flunk the test later.

Look, I'll stop, even though there's more. The point is Jesus claimed to be perfectly God and that He came down into man, perfectly Man, in flesh, to redeem mankind.

Now, why is the Incarnation important? Firstly, to fulfill the covenants that God made with man, salvation for all who would believe in the Son of God, the seed of woman. Secondly, the Law of the Old Testament *must* be fulfilled. Many Christians teach that we are not *under* the Law of the Old Testament, and while this is true, it is probably more correct to say: we are living under a *completed* Law through Jesus Christ.

This shows that the principles of the Law are, indeed, still there—they weren't done away with, just fulfilled by Christ. And by living *in* Christ, because He fulfilled and completed the Law, we enter into His right-standing. See the subtle difference?

That doesn't mean we must complete the Law, for we cannot—it is humanly impossible, and requires the influence of deity (Christ living inside us through His Spirit) to justify every aspect of the Law. This is why you and I don't sacrifice lambs on Yom Kippur. This is why you and I can eat bacon (if we choose to.) And this is why you and I are considered blameless before the Father.

It is not by any works on our behalf, but justification by faith in the blood of Jesus Christ. But to what are we justified against? The Law. If the Law went away, we would have nothing by which to be justified against, and the works of Christ would become meaningless. The Law is not thrown away, it is fulfilled in believing on Jesus Christ for salvation.

Again, read Matthew 5:17. Now, I know people looking for an argument will cite Ephesians 2:14-15 as proof that Jesus "did away" with the Law. But note the context Paul is speaking in: the separation of the Gentiles from the Jews by the Law, and that Christ—through His fulfillment of the Law—removed that enmity that separated Jew from "not Jew," which was caused by the separation of the Law. And He thereby created one Body of Christians, neither Jew nor Greek, bond nor free, male nor female (Galatians 3:28)—just one Body in Christ whereby we both (Jew and Gentile) have access to the same Father by the same Spirit. This is why in the very next sentence Paul goes on to say we are fellow citizens of the household of God—both believing (completed) Jew and believing Gentile.

God is holy, and as such requires holiness from His creation. God instituted the Law to convict man of his sin, and required that Man fulfill the punishment for that Law. Lastly, it was important that God reveal Himself in a way that could not be accomplished by the Law, but only through Jesus Christ in the revelation of a New Covenant between Himself and mankind. Jesus showed us the Father, and how we as followers of Him are to act—this includes moving in the miraculous!

Jesus showed mankind that God had always planned for His creation to live a sinless life; and that through His fulfillment of the Law in every perfect facet, His death as the atonement for sin, and His triumphant overcoming of Death (the result of sin) in His resurrection: Jesus showed the power of the enemy, the workings of Satan, were destroyed.

PERFECTLY SINLESS

We've established the Incarnation and touched on the dual natures within Jesus Christ—which we'll more fully flush out in a second. But before we do, let's drive home this truth that Jesus was unreservedly and unconditionally sinless. The only way for Jesus to be the Savior of all mankind is if He, as fully Man, could stand before God the Father and unequivocally state, "I have never sinned. My innocent blood was shed for sin, for the payment Your Law requires: that the guiltless must stand for the guilty. Therefore, forgive these people that believe in My ability to make payment for them."

And the Father said, "Okay. I am satisfied; I accept them through You."

If Christ had been a sinner, He would have needed a Savior. He could have died for His *own* sin, but not ours. The very crux of Christianity is rooted in the sinlessness (made-up word; I do that a lot!) of Jesus.

The only way to be sinless is to be perfect in every single facet of God's will. It must be 100% or nothing at all. Absolutely no deviation is acceptable. God is holy. His created beings (that's us) are required by their Creator to be perfect in fulfilling His will. Any departure from that will, no matter how slight, is sin. So therefore, Jesus not only had to be sinless in action—but even in what He thought and said. He had to be Perfect.

Some Christians erroneously believe Jesus' flesh was sinful—but not His spirit. They talk about Romans 8:3-4:

> "For what the law could not do in that it was weak through the flesh, God did by sending His own Son in the likeness of sinful flesh, on account of sin: He condemned sin in the flesh, that the righteous requirement of the law might be fulfilled in us who do not walk according to the flesh but according to the Spirit."

But it's that one little word "likeness" that shoots this theory out of the water. Christ's flesh was not "sinful flesh" but in the "likeness" of sinful flesh. That is the Greek *homoioma* (Strong's #3667, "ho-MOY-oh-mah") and it means, "that which has been made after the likeness of something; a figure, image, representation; likeness; resemblance, such as amounts almost to equality or identity."

See, in its original state, the body is not inherently sinful by itself. Sin has encroached upon the body (flesh); it is a parasite, not an elemental component of flesh. It attaches to flesh and corrupts it.

Jesus had real flesh, just like Adam had real flesh, just like you and me. The distinction is that there was no sin-principle, no sin nature, inside Jesus, just like Adam used to have before he sinned, just like we *would've* had if there had been no Original Sin. But Jesus' body was made in the "likeness" of sinful flesh, yet it was flesh that had no sin nature.

Okay, so let's discard this hypothesis. Where does that leave us? Either a) Jesus had the ability to sin but chose not to; or that b) He was incapable of sinning.

This is a major source of contention, even among Christians. I personally believe it is Option B, and I will show you why. However, I'm not here to start some holy war with those people who believe it is Option A. We shouldn't part as enemies over this, as long as we all agree, either in Option A or B, that whether Jesus *couldn't* sin, or whether Jesus *wouldn't* sin, the unarguable point that is not open to debate is that Jesus *didn't* sin.

So the Option A people point out that if Jesus Christ couldn't sin, what was the point of Satan testing Him? How can He be our great Example as an overcomer if the temptations were "staged" anyway?

These are valid questions I'm sure each of you has asked at one point in time. But let's identify *how* Christ was tempted.

> "Let no one say when he is tempted, 'I am tempted by God'; for God cannot be tempted by evil, nor does He Himself tempt anyone. But each one is tempted when he is drawn away by his own desires and enticed."
>
> (James 1:13-14)

Since Jesus was fully God, and since God cannot be tempted with evil, it is wrong to say Jesus was tempted in His deity. However, let's also recall He is fully Man and "...that He Himself has suffered, being tempted, He is able to aid those who are tempted." (Hebrews 2:18)

Otherwise, if Christ wasn't tempted the author of Hebrews couldn't have gone on to say, "For we do not have a High Priest who cannot sympathize with our weaknesses, but was in all points tempted as we are, yet without sin." It's important to accept that Jesus was tempted in every facet like us, except or apart from sin.

What this means is Jesus' temptation was *external* in nature; not internal. It is from without that He was tempted, not within, because He had no inherent sin nature. Jesus was tempted by Satan from the outside, not by His sin nature on the inside. We are tempted in both manners, outwardly and inwardly.

I've taught it like this: Jesus was confronted with thoughts of evil, but never had an evil thought. Satan showed Him evil things, but Jesus never thought up evil on His own.

Now, this means that Jesus—having a perfect dual nature—would feel the temptation even more acutely than we. Imagine if you'd never known sin, how horrified you would be by it. It would turn your stomach. Imagine if for all eternity past and present you'd never known one second apart from your relationship with the Father in heaven. And then being bodily tortured and hanged (it's hanged, not hung; people are hanged, pictures are hung) on a cross, the Father forsaking you.

Since Christ was unable to sin, imagine the impact of being made sin. (2 Corinthians 5:21)

Picture if you had been born with fire inside your body, would you be as concerned of fire outside your body? No, it was already in you from the start. But since we don't have fire inside our bodies, we are careful not to let fire touch our bodies on the outside. We do not want to be burned and inherently are repulsed from flames.

Jesus suffered what is termed "sinless infirmities." He was hungry; He was tired (although He was *never* sick); He was persecuted and beaten. In all this, Jesus was tested by His Father—as we are tested (not tempted.) To test, or to try, just means to "prove worthy."

> "Beloved, do not think it strange concerning the fiery trial which is to try you, as though some strange thing happened to you; but rejoice to the extent that you partake of Christ's sufferings, that when His glory is revealed, you may also be glad with exceeding joy. If you are reproached for the name of Christ, blessed are you, for the Spirit of glory and of God rests upon you. On their part He is blasphemed, but on your part He is glorified."
> (1 Peter 4:12-14)

The Lord was externally tempted by Satan to worship him, to champion His own will over God's, to feed His bodily hunger by usurping His anointing to turn stones into bread. So just like us, Jesus was tempted spirit, soul and body, only from an external source.

Jesus was tempted as a Man, not as God. Jesus conquered these temptations as Man, being fully Man. Yet, because of His divine nature assisting the human nature, He overcame the enemy by quoting God's Word. It takes the divine nature strengthening the human nature to overcome the temptation of the world. This is why Christ must live inside you for you to be able to "fulfill" the Law.

Thankfully, as being born-again, we are partakers of that divine nature of Christ; our natures are changed and we, too, can overcome. (2 Peter 1:4) I'm not saying we become God (that's humanism and is blasphemy.) I am saying we become godly (God-like) because of our engrafting into God's life through Jesus Christ. That is why we call ourselves Christians—"little Christs."

Since Jesus was fully God, it was impossible for Him to sin. Since He was fully Man, He was tempted and tested as we are. Some people would argue He could have sinned in His humanity, but not in His deity. However, even though His dual natures are distinct, they are inseparable. In the body of Jesus, one doesn't exist apart from the other. Therefore, to say "part" of Jesus could sin, is to say "all" of Jesus could sin. And therefore, undoing His divinity, making the entire effect of the cross of no consequence.

Okay, so I guess, really, I'm saying the Option A people are wrong. Sorry...

In any case, we as Christians *must* accept that Jesus Christ was sinless, whether He couldn't or wouldn't. He Himself said He was sinless. His Father was "well pleased" with all His actions. The apostles said He was sinless. Demons testified He was holy. The Old Testament taught sin offerings must be sinless (perfect, without spot or blemish.) Now I know you want scriptures here, so give me a minute to dig 'em all up for you. Got your pen ready to underline? Great. Here we go:

Exodus 12:5; Leviticus 4:3, 22:21; Numbers 19:2; Matthew 3:17, 8:29, 17:5; Mark 1:24; Luke 4:34; John 8:46, 14:30; 2 Corinthians 5:21; Hebrews 7:26, 9:14; 1 Peter 1:19, 2:21-22; 1 John 3:3-5.

Whew! That's a lot of typing. My hands hurt. Break time!

Okay, I'm back. One more thing I want to point out, and we'll move on. Jesus has now ascended to the right hand of the Father. He possesses a glorified body; He was the first to receive one, and we all eagerly await our own glorified body at His second coming. (For reference, go check out the whole last half of 1 Corinthians 15, Philippians 3:21, and 1 Thessalonians 4:15-18.) For all the rest of eternity (that's a long time), Jesus will always be fully God and fully Man. It is the requirement of our acceptance before the Father. He will always be our Mediator. And without Him, we are all doomed to hell.

No matter what, fifty bazillion years from now, we will simply be redeemed souls, and He will still be fully Man and fully God, still in a glorified body. He has permanently attached Himself to mankind. What a tremendous act of LOVE!

Jesus loves us so much that He would condescend forever to be fully Man and fully God in one glorified body. Powerful thought, huh? Perfect.

Because of His glorified state now, Jesus is beyond temptation and testing; He no longer suffers human weakness like hunger or tiredness. He is the First of what we will all follow suit one day; praise His name!

All right, so let's lay this all to rest, shall we? And let's talk at greater length about Christ's deity.

THREE O'S OF PERFECT GODNESS

As Jesus on this earth, He retained His complete deity. He remained fully God, possessing a divine nature; otherwise, the bridge between the two (God and man) could not have been maintained. So this means even on earth, Jesus was/is omniscient (all-knowing), omnipresent (everywhere present), omnipotent (all-powerful.) He was/is immutable; that means "wholly unchangeable forever." He was/is eternally self-existent—this is called aseity (Latin, "from self")—(I AM that I AM: I AM He who causes everything else to be; Exodus 3:14; John 8:58), and as such can offer eternality to those who believe in Him as God—the eternal life we have is in *HIS* eternal life as deity, and apart from His eternal life, we have none.

Lest people think I'm making this up, let's refer to scripture.

"But Jesus did not commit Himself to them, because He knew all men, and had no need that anyone should testify of man, for He knew what was in man." (John 2:24-25) This means He was/is all-knowing in His divine nature; this is why He "knew all things that would come upon Him." (John 18:4)

"No one has ascended to heaven but He who came down from heaven, that is, the Son of Man who is in heaven." (John 3:13) Omnipresent, in heaven and on earth simultaneously. This is what He means by "I am there in the midst of them," (Matthew 18:20) and, "I am with you always." (Matthew 28:20) He is everywhere, all at once.

Keep in mind all of this refers to Christ's divine nature—yes, of course, His flesh body was in one place at one time (fully Man.) Christ chose to limit His rights to act as deity while on the earth— we will explain this in just a moment. But for now, as one brief example, Jesus did not know Nathanael was sitting under the fig tree (John 1:48) because He was operating omnisciently—even though His divine nature was/is omniscient. He was reliant upon the Holy Spirit to operate in a word of knowledge.

> "If I do not do the works of My Father, do not believe Me; but if I do, though you do not believe Me, believe the works, that you may know and believe that the Father is in Me, and I in Him."
>
> (John 10:37-38)

Jesus did works that no one else did (John 15:24); He expected people to believe in His power based on those works (John 14:11); and these works bore witness of Him. (John 10:25) Jesus was omnipotent in His divine nature as fully God, but as fully Man He emptied Himself: that is, He did not abdicate His divine nature, but He humbled Himself and condescended to become a servant to humanity, utterly reliant upon His Father and the anointing of God's Spirit, to execute only His Father's will in every facet, at every time (perfectly!), with only the authority the Father delegated to Him. (John 5:30) He only performed that which He *saw* (omniscience, again) His Father do in heaven. (John 5:19)

Jesus as fully Man was dependent upon the anointing (Messiah and Christ mean "anointed one") of the Holy Spirit. See Acts 10:38, then Luke 4:14 and just a bit lower when He quotes Isaiah, "He has anointed Me."

Further, Jesus did this of His own freewill. It is because of God's love (John 3:16) that He offered His life for mankind. "No one takes it from Me, but I lay it down of Myself. I have power to lay it down, and I have power to take it again. This command I have received from My Father." (John 10:18)

Let's sum all this up from an absolutely beautiful (perfect!) passage of scripture.

> "...who, being in the form of God, did not consider it robbery to be equal with God, but made Himself of no reputation, taking the form of a bondservant, and coming in the likeness of men. And being found in appearance as a man, He humbled Himself and became obedient to the point of death, even the death of the cross."
>
> (Philippians 2:6-8)

As fully God, Jesus cannot change. (Hebrews 13:8) He is Perfect. It is error to say that Jesus stopped being God, or emptied Himself of divinity, while on the earth. It isn't that God changed Himself into a man; rather, He took on the nature (likeness) of man, but didn't stop being God. When we talk about "self-emptying" we mean that Jesus set aside His rights as God—His privilege to act independently as deity—and relied fully on His Father in heaven, becoming dependent on the Father's will when executing any of His godly manifestation through the power of the Holy Spirit. See why it's dangerous to downplay the Trinity?

Let me point out Matthew 24:36. In this scripture, Jesus is saying that no one knows, except the Father in heaven, when the second coming will be. Some manuscripts say, "nor the Son;" the King James leaves it out. But I bring this up to point out that if the Son didn't know while He was on earth, being omniscient, it shows He relied unreservedly on the Father's insight, only revealing that which the Father showed Him—His will was completely subjected to the Father's. (Obviously Jesus knows *now* if He didn't know *then* while on earth.) The intention is to show that if the Father said, "No;" Jesus said, "Okay." If the Father said, "Yes;" Jesus said, "Okay." Again, perfect.

There's a technical name for all of this. In Philippians 2:7, Paul uses the phrase, "Made Himself of no reputation." That Greek word is *kenoo* (Strong's #2758, "ken-AH-oh") and it means "to make empty." So theologians call this the "Kenosis" of Christ.

Some people argue Kenosis goes against Hypostatic Union. Hypostasis means "foundation, underpinning"—the existence of something. It means, to us, that Jesus on earth was fully God, and fully Man, at the same time in one "hypostasis." So some people would call Kenosis a theory and dispute that it is contrary for Jesus to empty Himself of Godness and yet retain Godness. (Godness is not a real word; I just made it up.) But really the confusion arises in the definition of "emptying."

We—and I hope you ('cause we're right; insert smiley face here)—maintain Jesus didn't empty Himself of His deity, but His rights to ACT as deity, only showing forth His divine nature as the Father willed, as in the case of the Transfiguration for one example (see Matthew 17:1-9; Mark 9:2-8; Luke 9:28-36; 2 Peter 1:16-18—no, I'm serious; go look these up!) We believe Kenosis and Hypostatic Union exist side-by-side.

Jesus Christ was/is God, now and forever. So much so, it convinced Doubting Thomas:

> "And after eight days His disciples were again inside, and Thomas with them. Jesus came, the doors being shut, and stood in the midst, and said, 'Peace to you!' Then He said to Thomas, 'Reach your finger here, and look at My hands; and reach your hand here, and put it into My side. Do not be unbelieving, but believing.' And Thomas answered and said to Him, 'My Lord and my God!'"
>
> (John 20:26-28)

PERFECT MANNESS

Manness is also a totally made up word; it gets a squiggly red line under it just like Godness—humanity is probably a better choice, but I like manness.

I believe we've established Jesus was fully God. But it's important to recognize the necessity of Jesus being fully Man. Not just because only a Man could stand as payment for the sins of man, but because as a Man, Jesus provides us with the Great Example about how we should operate as Christians. As truth warriors of the supernatural, our search for such release comes only from our understanding of how the Man operated on this earth. Jesus showed us how to use the anointing.

Some people called Him the Son of David, showing His earthly right to the Judaic throne. Some people called Him the Son of God, showing His divinity as being the only begotten of the Father. But the term that Jesus most often used to refer to Himself was the Son of Man. That phrase is used eighty-something times in the New Testament, more than seventy times in the Gospels alone, and usually by Jesus Himself. (I'm not going to argue with people who question whether Jesus meant Himself when He said Son of Man—it's a waste of time. Let's assume I'm right, and it's a title He uses for Himself.)

We don't need to discourse on the appropriateness, or deep, hidden meaning of "Son of Man." Read Daniel 7 and come to your own conclusions, hermeneutically.

Realistically, and simplistically, Jesus was identifying with the human race and called Himself a Man. He was born of a human mother, whom He acknowledged and honored. He grew up just like every other human child; He learned and worked. He was of Jewish nationality (not a White Anglo Saxon Protestant, ha ha!) He possessed a real flesh-and-bone body, with blood—albeit special blood created by the Father. He had a spirit. He had a mind, will (which was completely subjected to the Father's) and emotions (all three of which we call a "soul.") Before His glorification, He was limited to one place in time and space; He grew in knowledge, from childhood to adulthood. He got hungry and ate; He got tired and slept. He was able to weep, laugh, get angry, jump, twirl and shout. He was able to feel sympathy for others. All the normal "human" stuff we'd expect from someone completely human.

Except for sin.

So why does this matter? What is the point of having two natures reside in one body?

To be the "new creation." To show us as humans the way to the Father, through Jesus. For the Messiah to be our great Example in all things, everything, fully revealing the Father's divine intent for our lives; His purpose for our existence. To be perfect. Complete and whole. It takes balance as a Christian to understand His dual nature (not dual personality)—to be doctrinally balanced, never forgetting that Jesus is fully God and fully Man. He is equal to the Father as God and subjected to the Father as Man; not either or, both! It is not a matter of confusion, but a revelation of the perfection that is found in Jesus Christ.

Only this kind of Person could be our Mediator of the new covenant of salvation through faith in this Person. If any one portion is thrown out of balance—too much reliance on His Godness, or too much emphasis on His manness—we can fall dangerously in error of corrupting the simplicity that is found in Jesus Christ, the God-Man.

As humans, it is important for us to keep everything centered in Christ. It all comes back to Him. Even as truth warriors of the supernatural, eager to express the glory of God to a hurting world, it all comes back to our understanding of Jesus as God and Man. We are enabled to have access to the might of the Father's throne through Jesus' Godness, don't forget that! Our sins are forgiven at the behest of Jesus' Godness. Lest we forget!

But also, let us recognize and understand that everything Jesus did in the name of releasing the glory of the Father on earth: all of His signs, wonders, miracles, prophetic words, healings, prayers, fastings, on and on; Jesus did these as a Man. A Man that was anointed by the Holy Spirit. Otherwise, how can we hope to attain to His works and the greater (in number) that He assures us we will do, through faith in Him? (John 14:12) If Jesus healed as God, or cast out demons as God—we have no great Example. The anointing of the Holy Spirit is for naught. Jesus' name is of no consequence in this day. The purpose of studying His Word, being released in a heavenly prayer language, activating our faith and stepping out to offer what the world is seeking, is completely worthless if Christ only did what Christ did as God.

Cessationists maintain that anointing is over. The season has passed, and people two thousand years ago (actually the Jews from the Old Testament!) had it so much better than we do. They had healing; they had deliverance; they had prophecy; they had a tangible, physical undeniable proof of Jesus' authority—even through His apostles.

But many today tell us this grace is over; they say there are no prophets, there is no healing (unless GOD does it sovereignly, apart from any action on man's behalf), there is no "tongues;" there is no personal anointing; no gifts of the Holy Spirit; no apostles; no manifestation of Jesus' authority, except as sovereign God, if He wills or deigns to save who He wants, deliver who He wants, raise who He wants from the dead. Why not just throw away the whole last half of your New Testament—if it doesn't apply to today?

Matter of fact, let's just toss out the Old Testament, too. Unless we all want to convert to Judaism, because at least, hey, they had a covenant of healing and provision!

They say we've moved on from all of that; we have evolved beyond a need for the anointing and grace works. Who are they?

They're wrong.

Jesus did what He did as a Man, to show us the way. To say to us, "You, too, can be anointed by My Spirit, approved by My Father. You, too, can preach the acceptable year of the Lord. You, too, can have signs, wonders and miracles backing up the validity of My Word. Go into all the world. Make disciples. Baptize them in My name, My Father's name, My Spirit's name. Teach them all that I have commanded. And behold, I'm with you. Even unto the end of the age." (See Matthew 28:16-20.)

What age has ended? Show me in a Bible—any translation. When has this stopped? What are we to observe in His commandments: salvation and nothing else? That's insulting to me, you and God! Has Jesus ceased being fully God and fully Man? Has Jesus ceased to be our great Example and Mediator? Has

131

He commanded us to ignore His actions? To demean His Spirit and the anointing?

Has Jesus changed?

No! Thank You, Lord!

As truth warriors, let me urge you in the strongest, most passionate way I can type: press into that understanding of Jesus as God, and Jesus as Man. And as a Man, let Him be your prime, only, singular example on *how* we should operate on a daily basis. If He healed, we should heal. If He delivered, we should deliver. If He prophesied, we should prophesy. And don't let *anyone* tell you otherwise.

Anything less is to be not perfect.

The Truth of Sin and Salvation

There are a bunch of technical terms theologians use when breaking down theology into its many categories. (The word *theology* means "study of God," but it doesn't always mean the study of the Christian God, Jehovah.)

Like *theology*, these terms are usually a Greek prefix attached to –ology (meaning "the study of"), like "biology" is the study of life. Or "cosmetology" is the study of beautification (that's arguable.) Or "Scientology" is the study of how to make millions of dollars from Hollywood stars. No, no, I'm joking there. It's actually the study of ancient alien colonization. (Well, sort of...)

Anyway, when we study the reality or existence of something that's called *ontology*. The origin of ontology comes from metaphysics, and does not necessarily mean the "study of the existence of God," although that is one facet of ontology—but it rather just means "the study of existence" in general. As in Descartes' "I think therefore I am" statement.

The concepts discussed in the previous chapter on the Truth of Jesus Christ is called Christology, and it's usually capitalized because it refers to a specific title "Christ," meaning "the Anointed One." (It's not His last name... that was "of Nazareth." Okay, I'll stop with the bad jokes.)

The Roman Catholics add a branch to Christology called Mariology, the study of Mary and her relationship to the Christ. It is almost as important as Christology to them, and they believe you cannot separate one from the other and arrive at a complete concept of Jesus Christ without both branches. And while we as Protestants hold Mary in high regard, as the human mother of Christ, we don't place nearly the emphasis on her as we do on Christology.

The main concepts of Christology are Christ's Personage (which we discussed at length in the last chapter), His dual nature, His deity and humanity; His birth, crucifixion and subsequent resurrection; His glorification and the authority in His name; and the offices which He performed in His earthly ministry and His ascendant position.

This is the so-called *munus triplex*. Everything sounds smarter in Latin. You'll recognize triplex as a house split into three very small apartments, or a movie theater with three screens. No, here it just means "three." *Munus* is an office one stands in (not an office one goes to work in.) Like one can stand in the "office of" a prophet, apostle, evangelist, pastor or teacher, according to Ephesians 4. It signifies a duty or obligation, a type of employment, a service or a burden one must perform.

The three offices Christ executes are as Prophet (Deuteronomy 18), Priest (Psalm 110) and King. (Psalm 2) How many know Jesus as the Word of God incarnate was the greatest Prophet, bringing the total thought (logos) of God the Father to the people? His passion, crucifixion and resurrection provide the means of coming unto the Father with Him as our High Priest. And His ascension position at the Father's right hand shows His eternal kingship over all creation; all authority has been given to King Jesus. (Matthew 28:18)

Every aspect of Christology falls under one of these three main categories. You would do well, as a truth warrior of the supernatural, to keep these three offices in mind whenever you administer Jesus to people. Salvation, inner healing, sanctification? Jesus as Priest. A word of encouragement, exhortation, comfort, knowledge, wisdom? Jesus as Prophet. Authority, sonship, dominion? Jesus as King. By accepting Christ, we are accepted into His royal priesthood, with all the same rights and privileges pertaining to such.

> "But you are a chosen generation, a royal priesthood, a holy nation, His own special people, that you may proclaim the praises of Him who called you out of darkness into His marvelous light..."
>
> (1 Peter 2:9)

The study of salvation is called *soteriology*, and technically any religion's "form" of salvation falls under this umbrella term. However, when we speak of it as Christians, we mean saving grace through belief in Jesus Christ as God, whose blood was shed for the forgiveness of sins, and is accepted by faith. (Romans 3:28)

TYPES OF SIN

The study of sin and its consequences is called *hamartiology*. The Greek word (Strong's #266, *hamartia*, "ham-ar-TEE-ah") means "error," or "missing the mark" as when an archer's arrow goes astray. The concept behind the word *hamartia* can also convey a foible, like a fatal flaw, a chink in the armor, an Achilles' heel. But we as Christians mean it in the biblical sense: a sin is anything that is a violation of God's revealed will. So thus, God says "don't murder" period—and if one murders, that is sin. There can be a sin of commission, knowingly committing a willful, rebellious act. There can also be a sin of omission.

"Therefore, to him who knows to do good and does not do it, to him it is sin." (James 4:17)

The book of Romans is probably the single greatest treatise on sin and salvation in the Bible. Truth warriors of the supernatural would do well to spend hours and hours, reading, re-reading, memorizing and meditating on Romans. Specifically Paul outlines the struggle of both types of sin: commission and omission in Chapter 7.

> "For we know that the law is spiritual, but I am carnal, sold under sin. For what I am doing, I do not understand. For what I will to do, that I do not practice; but what I hate, that I do. If, then, I do what I will not to do, I agree with the law that it is good. But now, it is no longer I who do it, but sin that dwells in me. For I know that in me (that is, in my flesh) nothing good dwells; for to will is present with me, but how to perform what is good I do not find. For the good that I will to do, I do not do; but the evil I will not to do, that I practice. Now if I do what I will not to do, it is no longer I who do it, but sin that dwells in me."
>
> (Romans 7:14-20)

This may seem like a difficult passage to modern readers. Try substituting "I will" with "I decide." The apostle is here lamenting doing what he knows he ought not to do (commission), as well as knowing what he ought to do, and not doing it (omission.) Both are sin. He is teaching in his flesh-man, he wars against sin still, and that his inward will is to do good always, but he fails sometimes.

To teach that the moment a person becomes a believer in Jesus Christ, they never sin, is error. By the fact that we are still human, in a flesh-and-bone body, sojourning in a world that is enslaved to the sin principle (though we are no longer "of this world;" see John 15:19; Romans 12:2) means that we war against sin.

Once we are born again, it is no longer in our nature to be callous toward sin, to be flippant; we are not slaves to sin. (Romans 6:20; John 8:34) The moment the Holy Spirit lives within our spirits, making us spiritually alive toward God, our spirits are saved from the *penalties* of sin. The "old man" (the spirit that is deadened toward God because of sin) is crucified with Christ, and we are raised from the dead spiritually into the newness of life (Romans 6:4), becoming new creations—that is, a new species of human. We call this being "born again."

This starts a new process in our lives wherein the born-again spirit-man, through the help of the Holy Spirit's indwelling, begins to combat and overcome the *powers* of sin. While we might stumble and fall short on occasion, we are no longer controlled by a sin nature. All propensity toward sin resides in our flesh-man (our mind, our wills, our emotions and our physical bodies.)

There is a distinction between the spirit-man and the flesh-man (comprising our soul and body.) Your spirit-man is saved the moment you believe in Christ's redeeming grace through His shed blood, and you confess this with your mouth. (Romans 10:9-10)

You must still continue to crucify your flesh-man with Christ in a progressive walk with Him. This is how we war against sin.

> "I say then: Walk in the Spirit, and you shall not fulfill the lust of the flesh. For the flesh lusts against the Spirit, and the Spirit against the flesh; and these are contrary to one another, so that you do not do the things that you wish. But if you are led by the Spirit, you are not under the law."
>
> Galatians 5:16-18

In Galatians 5, Paul clearly outlines the distinction between the fleshly and the spiritual. The fruit of the Spirit is the hallmark of godly living—overcoming the power of sin in our walk. Note that the works of the flesh are organized by three facets of sin: against God, against others, against ourselves. As we put down the flesh-man, we overcome the works of the flesh, and the Spirit puts His fruit in its place.

Finally, when we meet the Lord in the air, our very bodies will become incorruptible (1 Corinthians 15:53-54), like Christ's, and we will be completely free from the very *presence* of sin for all eternity.

Now, pay attention: this doesn't mean that while we live on this earth we "have" to sin because we struggle against our flesh-man—it means we war against it, and it is a war we can win by the strengthening of the Holy Spirit living within us.

Still, even if we as Christians, have gotten to a place where we do not sin in our actions—it is still possible for us to sin in our inactions, and we must be aware of this notion.

The Lord outlined these concepts with the parable of the Good Samaritan. (Luke 10) By ignoring what we know we should do (help a person in need, in this case)—we have sinned by omitting our correct duty. Those who passed by the beaten man were as guilty as the robbers themselves. They were just as lawless as the thieves. "Whoever commits sin also commits lawlessness, and sin is lawlessness." (1 John 3:4)

What is so frightening about an ultra-grace doctrine is that in its most extreme form, it leads to a callousness, an indifference, toward sin. And we often forget—even if our acts (commission) are 100% perfect always (and I've yet to meet a human being who's attained)—that by knowing to do good and doing it not, we have sinned. And I'm sorry, we all neglect to do good from time to time, I don't care who you are. That is not an excuse to give up and stop warring against complacency and omission (see Romans 6:1-2.) Let us not weary in doing good! (Galatians 6:9)

But rather, we need to be aware we all have areas in our lives that are not perfectly aligned to the will of God 100% of the time—and therefore, that is sin.

Space fails me to copy the whole of Matthew 5, but I strongly urge you (even if you think you've read it 1,000 times) to read it a thousand more.

Jesus taught that even pervasive *thoughts* are sin, whether or not those thoughts are acted upon. Lust is adultery in the heart. Unjust anger is murder in the heart. Now, of course, Jesus did not say thinking of murder means just go ahead and do it (commit the actual act)—that's stupidity in its highest form.

Of course, there is a distinction between thinking of a sin and actually doing a sin—but the consequences before God and the need for forgiveness (repentance) remain the same, in thought or in deed.

We know that thought germinates into activity, for, "Then, when desire has conceived, it gives birth to sin; and sin, when it is full-grown, brings forth death." (James 1:15)

See, in Matthew 5, Jesus was showing that sin stems from iniquity. Iniquity means to be "bent" toward sin. So, if adultery is the committed act of sin, inward lust is the iniquity, the driving force behind the sin. If being an alcoholic is a sin of commission, the iniquity of addiction is the motivating principle behind the act. Jesus said it was all sin, and it must all be uprooted. (Matthew 3:10)

To say once we are born-again, we no longer sin, or that we do not war against sin in our flesh-man, is a form of humanism and heresy—wherein, we become a god unto ourselves. For if there was no sin in our lives after we are born-again, at some point in time, we would cease to need a Savior. Our righteousness would be complete in ourselves. I go to painstaking lengths in *Panoramic Seer* about this serious mistaken notion, and again, I encourage you to really study this concept out.

I am not saying that our past sins are not forgiven, nor am I saying we "must" sin—for once we are born again, it is not in our nature to continuously live in aberrant, habitual sin (committing or omitting.) But to say we never need repent again as long as we're on this earth—that's a very dangerous notion. I believe in a lifestyle of repentance, a constant attitude of contrition, and acceptance of grace as a costly sacrifice on behalf of God Almighty. I do not live in condemnation or over-regret concerning sins of the past—but neither do I neglect to quickly confess sins in the present—nor do I treat lightly sins of the future.

CONTINUING SALVATION

The correct doctrine concerning salvation is a present, continuous activity. When you repented (changed your mind toward sin) and became saved, your spirit was born-again (made alive toward God)—this is an act of grace and cannot be earned no matter what you do or don't do. It is a miracle on the behalf of God through the blood of Jesus Christ. This is called justification. You and the Lord are square. Your past sins are forgiven, and the Holy Spirit takes up residence within your spirit—you are alive in Christ and are called a "new creation."

Throughout the course of your born-again life, the Holy Spirit begins to teach you how to live like God demands (holy.) This does not mean you cannot sin, nor that you do not sin, but rather the Spirit as Teacher and Helper, through illuminating the Word (studying the Bible), begins to work with you on areas of your life that may have roots of iniquity. This is called sanctification—being set apart to live how God expects you to live.

Should you die, or if the Lord returns in your lifetime, in the future of eternity you will then be given a glorified body, of the kind Jesus has now. This body is incorruptible and free from the very presence of sin. It is at this time that you are removed from sin, you will no longer sin, commission, omission, in thought or in deed. This is called glorification.

Do you want to know what I think is one of the single greatest factors that prohibits God's people (and the people of the world for that matter) from experiencing the supernatural truth of healing and wholeness in this life? I'm glad you asked.

Ready for this? It's unconfessed sin.

I know because I pray with literally thousands of people every year for some kind of healing, emotional or physical. Being a prophetic kinda guy, the Lord most often reveals the hindrance to that healing stems from a sin issue.

Now don't worry, God doesn't show all the little sordid details, that's between you and Him. Nor do I care to know. And quite truthfully, it's not even committed sins a lot of the time—most often, it's omitted sins, sometimes even stemming from someone just simply not *knowing*. But a root of iniquity, even with no physical outward manifestation of sin, can give a trespass right, an open door, a generational curse (I'm sure you've heard all these terms before), so on and so forth. And I'll be honest, the enemy will take whatever it can get. This is why we are admonished to give no place to the devil (Ephesians 4:27): just an inch, and he'll take a mile, to bust out an old cliché.

One of the greatest doctrines of truth that I can convey to you in this book is the absolute necessity of dealing with sin, omitted or committed, in your life. Give no part to sin. Resist the devil (and you *can* resist him!) and he will flee. (James 4:7) You do *not* have to give into temptation no matter what your mind tells you.

If and when you sin, don't let it go. Don't ignore it, don't push it down, don't talk yourself out of needing to ask for forgiveness and to repent. Do it quickly, don't harbor it out of some false sense of self-pity or uncaring attitude towards it. This is how iniquity sets in. We have grace for this very reason—not to continue sinning, but to take care of it, should we stumble, and then move on. This is why Jesus told the woman in John 8:11, "Go and sin no more." In other words, stop it. Don't keep doing this.

I'm all about grace, thank God for it. But we cannot take it for granted. I recall a comment from a well-known author who once said he enjoyed "the wastefulness of grace." Now, I know what he means—grace is unmerited, we don't deserve it. But to say it's *wasteful*; that's a sad, poor choice of words. Grace came at a very costly price, and it should never be wasted... You've probably seen the bumper stickers: "Freedom is not free." Same idea here. The pardon of grace was paid with great expense. You are a pearl of great price (Matthew 13:46) that Jesus purchased with every drop of His blood and sweat and tears. Don't cast yourself before swine. (Matthew 7:6) I'll leave it at that.

Okay, so again, Catholicism teaches there are different kinds of sins apart from commission and omission: there are ones that do not jeopardize salvation (venial) and ones that do (mortal.) Venial sins are "forgiven" by acts of penance (either in this life or in purgatory.) Mortal sins send someone to hell unless they are confessed.

Now, for Protestant Christianity there is usually not quite so much of a distinction, and yet, most Protestants do recognize, "All unrighteousness is sin, and there is sin not leading to death." (1 John 5:17)

> "And Jesus answered and said to them, 'Do you suppose that these Galileans were worse sinners than all other Galileans, because they suffered such things? I tell you, no; but unless you repent you will all likewise perish.'"
>
> (Luke 13:2-3)

All sin needs to be cleansed, no matter how small, but there are many varying viewpoints on how a sin affects a Protestant Christian, ranging all the way from one sin means you lose your salvation and go to hell (this is usually in very strict religious groups, a couple examples being Nazarene, Mennonite, etc.)—all the way to you can sin as much as you want and still go to heaven, because once saved, always saved. These groups usually teach some form of: "all your sins you have committed and will ever commit were forgiven the moment you got saved."

Now, to be fair, most denominations don't say "you can do whatever you want and still get to heaven"—but they do attest to a once saved, always saved concept, arguing that if you lose your salvation, you weren't really saved to begin with. And that if you truly are saved you won't want to "do whatever you want" in the first place.

I bet you want to know what I believe, right? Well, I'm not gonna tell you.

No, I'm joking. As with most controversial subjects in Christianity, I tend to take a middle of the road approach. There is an element of truth to both sides of the equation. I *do* believe a Christian can reject the gift of salvation by living continuously in unconfessed, habitual sin. However, I think one has to really *work* at it to lose one's salvation.

And there is some truth to the notion that if you're truly saved (what Maria Woodworth-Etter called "brightly converted"), you wouldn't want to live in a continuous state of unrepentant sins of habit in the first place.

But since you and I couldn't possibly know when that moment occurs, don't push it. Grace is *not* about how much you can get away with. It is the means by which you can overcome.

To say we need never to repent again after the initial acceptance of the gift of salvation is to abdicate our responsibility before God to live a holy life. That very stance is a sin of omission, see? For we *should* know to do good (repentance is a good action) and we do it not.

Lastly, I'll briefly point out the Unforgiveable Sin that Jesus talks about in Matthew 12:31. The Bible makes it clear that *every* sin a person can commit—no matter how vile, disgusting, base or perverted—can also be forgiven. Except one.

So, the misconception many people have, "God can't forgive me—you don't know the things that I've done," is about the most foolish statement a person can make, and it is one that will send them to hell.

Yes, there is truth to the notion that at some point in time, God gives a sinner over to a reprobate mind (Romans 1:27-29) and their conscience becomes seared. (1 Timothy 4:2) But this doesn't mean they *can't* get saved; it's just that they most likely won't. They have made their decision. There is only so many times a person can reject the truth of Jesus Christ, before their heart becomes hardened. In these cases, it is very difficult (I won't say impossible) for these people to come (or return) to Christ. Only God knows at what point in time a person has committed a sin unto death (again, 1 John 5:16.)

Most often, the Lord will—and this is an act of *love*, even though it sounds callous—"deliver such a one to Satan for the destruction of the flesh, that his spirit may be saved in the day of the Lord Jesus." (1 Corinthians 5:5) God tries very hard to get people to come to Him—even if their decisions to stubbornly reject Him create a living hell for them. Whatever it takes, the Lord will permit, for the alternative is eternity in damnation. Some come easily to Him, some come kicking and screaming, but it's the ones who aren't coming to Him at all that concern Him the most—and should concern us as well.

Okay, I got a little off track. All of that is *not* talking about the Unpardonable Sin. No matter what a person has done, it will be forgiven if they just repent. Except blasphemy against the Holy Spirit.

Now, look this isn't offhand, glib blasphemy. The context is the Pharisees saying the supernatural works of Jesus were done under the authority and power of the Lord of the Flies

(Beelzebub.) Whether you believe Beelzebub refers specifically to Satan or to one of the fallen angels—the point is, these Jewish religious leaders were claiming Christ's anointing was from hell, not heaven.

This is a level of mockery rarely seen—to call that which is holy, unholy, and that which is unholy, holy. To take Someone as precious as the Spirit (who is holy) and call Him a worker of the devil—well, my friends, there's not that many of us out there in the world who've gone *that* far off the deep end.

Jesus points out the stupidity of this notion by saying basically, "How does the devil cast out the devil?" Duh. But these *ultra-religious* (not "worldly sinners") had crossed a line—they'd become so dull, so seared, so mired in false religiosity that they couldn't even tell who could cast out who. This is a rare case. One has to work to get to this position of deception where they commit the Unpardonable Sin. It doesn't happen overnight.

I have met dozens of well-meaning Christians who worried and fretted over this. "When I was a sinner, I made fun of the Holy Spirit, when I saw Benny Hinn on TV. What if I've committed the Unpardonable Sin?"

Sometimes it's Ernest Angley, but their concern is the same.

I always respond, "Does that bother you, if you committed the Unpardonable Sin? Do you feel bad about that?"

"Yes!"

"Then you haven't committed it. Don't worry. 'Cause if you had, you wouldn't care."

Okay, a brief insert here for further clarification on the "sin unto death." I've touched on it above, but I felt I should really clarify the distinction between the "Unpardonable Sin" and "the sin unto death." So let me just re-quote the passage here:

> "If anyone sees his brother sinning a sin which does not lead to death, he will ask, and He will give him life for those who commit sin not leading to death. There is sin leading to death. I do not say that he should pray about that. All unrighteousness is sin, and there is sin not leading to death."
>
> (1 John 5:16-17)

Some people, usually from a once-saved, always-saved background, believe the "sin unto death" is just simply the sin of unbelief: "I reject Christ, therefore I go to hell." Sin leading to death because the person fails to accept Christ. And I can see this, it makes sense. Except, in the context of the passage above, John is talking about "a brother"—someone already believing in Christ—and doesn't make the distinction that he's then talking about a disbeliever in the "there is sin leading to death" comment.

So, I think the "sin unto death" can be rendered a little deeper than just "ignoring or disbelieving Christ as the Savior." Especially in light of the passage from Hebrews 6, which is one of the most well-known chapters because it's the basis for basic Christian foundation. Yet, I think sometimes we can tend to gloss over this part of the chapter:

> "For it is impossible for those who were once enlightened, and have tasted the heavenly gift, and have become partakers of the Holy Spirit, and have tasted the good word of God and the powers of the age to come, if they fall away, to renew them again to repentance, since they crucify again for themselves the Son of God, and put Him to an open shame. For the earth which drinks in the rain that often comes upon it, and bears herbs useful for those by whom it is cultivated, receives blessing from God; but if it bears thorns and briers, it is rejected and near to being cursed, whose end is to be burned."
>
> (Hebrews 6:4-8)

Now, I've heard some people argue this isn't included or phrased this way in some translations, but I say that's garbage. Give me a break. This isn't some minor translation difference or some obscure, poetic reference in the Old Testament that has no eternal bearing if we have a difference of opinion. This is salvation we're talking about here. The whole crux of the Bible, the reason for its existence. We'd better get *this* right at least! As an element of faith in the inerrancy of the Bible we're reading (and we're not talking "Bob's Translation" here—this *is* the King James) we must believe this is important enough, and that God is thorough enough, to have this concept included.

Let's take me as an example here. James Maloney, full-time minister for forty years, written many books on Christian doctrine, moved in the gifts of the Spirit as the Lord willed, preached to many, many thousands, taught in Bible schools for, like, twenty years. Look, I'm not boasting in myself—this is the ministry the Lord has entrusted to me. But that's the point—He's *entrusted* it to me. Don't mess this up, James!

So let's say I decide to *habitually* reject Christ. I mean, a total lifestyle change—I go back into the world; I'm cheating on my wife and unrepentant; I'm intentionally deceiving people when I stand behind the pulpit; I'm consistently lying and stealing and doing all the things that *every* Christian agrees is "wrong." On a habitual basis, keep in mind. I'm not talking about people who make mistakes and are truly broken, humble and repenting—changing their minds toward sin, endeavoring to overcome and not fall again.

(Don't worry, we're speaking hypothetically here to make a point. I'm *not* doing those things, just to be real clear...)

I'm talking about ministers and sound, strong Christians who have known the "right way"—mature Christians (not the newly saved)—who continuously reject and "crucify Christ again" with their blatant, habitual sin.

I believe it is possible for these kinds of people to commit the sin unto death, rare as it may be. That is, they can lose their salvation, or reject it, or become so hardened in sin that they can't repent. However way you want to term it.

A minister acquaintance was once given a visitation from the Lord. (Most of you will know of whom I speak.) In this open vision, the Lord showed this brother a person who over the course of many years, in spite of what they knew to be right, continuously rejected that knowledge of Christ by wantonly remaining in gross, habitual sin—bad stuff. Even still the Lord said this person, at any given point in time could have repented and would've been restored. This person over a long period of time became obsessed with evil thoughts that came against them, and eventually gave way to those "evil thoughts," so that they dropped down into their spirit and became "thoughts of evil."

See the difference? Evil thoughts are outside that come against. Thoughts of evil are your own made up desires of sin which come from the inside.

There came a point in this person's life that they had rejected Christ so utterly, even knowing what He expected of them as a mature Christian, that Jesus told our brother who was receiving this vision: the person had committed the sin unto death and couldn't be restored. Now, perhaps your theology doesn't handle that, so let's soften that and say the person *wouldn't* be restored—that, in themselves, they'd lost the ability to come back to Christ, whether Christ would've accepted them back or not. However way you wish to look at it, the point is, this person was lost. And that's terribly, terribly sad.

None of us should live in fear of sin. But we should all live in reverential fear of the Lord and seek to remain soft, malleable, teachable, humble, broken and contrite before Him. No one can know at what point in time they've reached that place of no return. The point is, don't play with fire; don't test it in the first place. Sometimes it's okay to err on the side of caution when it comes to eternity!

But hey, this is not you! You are a truth warrior of the supernatural. We're not talking about you! Like the author of Hebrews goes on to state, I am completely:

> "...confident of better things concerning you, yes, things that accompany salvation, though we speak in this manner. For God is not unjust to forget your work and labor of love which you have shown toward His name, in that you have ministered to the saints, and do minister. And we desire that each one of you show the same diligence to the full assurance of hope until the end, that you do not become sluggish, but imitate those who through faith and patience inherit the promises."
>
> (Hebrews 6:9-12)

ORIGINAL SIN

The doctrine of Original Sin is one that most of mainstream Christianity (Catholic and Protestant) adheres to. It is basically the concept that due to Adam's sin in disobeying God concerning the fruit of the Tree of Knowledge of Good and Evil, all subsequent members of the human race have inherited Adam's sin nature, thereby being born in sin and deadened spiritually toward God.

There, as usual, are varying degrees of what the notion of Original Sin means to an individual person. One notion has been accredited to a monk named Pelagius, who may or may not have agreed with several of the doctrines that were given in his name. But, it is generally attributed to him that Pelagius taught mankind did not inherit Adam's sin nature but was rather influenced toward sin by the bad example Adam presented.

On the opposite side, Calvinists (although again John Calvin didn't agree with everything purported in his name) hold that all people inherit a sin nature based on Adam's original sin, and further they receive the punishment due to Adam because of this inherited nature. In other words, everyone is guilty of Adam's sin, and their own.

Another approach held by Arminians (yet again, not everything the Arminians hold as true is strictly from Jacobus Arminius himself) is that while mankind did inherit a natural propensity toward sin due to Adam's fall, they are not held strictly accountable for his sin, rather they have enough sin in their own stead to condemn them. This concept is sometimes linked to Semipelagianism (kind of a hybrid form of Pelagianism) and prevenient grace (grace apart from human decision, whether or not that grace can be accepted or rejected by human freewill.)

The doctrine of an inherited sin nature due to Adam's fall is sometimes called federal headship—as in, Adam was the father of the whole human race and as such was our first representative before God. He failed, so we fail. Conversely, Jesus is the last Adam and as such serves as our Head and representative before God, for those who believe in Him.

Now, a lot of this is splitting hairs. That doesn't mean it's entirely unimportant, but we could spend pages and pages going back and forth outlining a hundred different -isms.

Whether sin is inherited or imputed or whatever, we as truth warriors must accept that all have sinned and have fallen short of the glory of God. (Romans 3:23) Again, Paul in Romans 5 pretty much outlines that everyone is guilty of transgression before God—and everyone needs a Savior found only in Jesus

Christ. Bottom line is God "now commands all men everywhere to repent." (Acts 17:30)

So whether you believe in a whole, partial, or non-inheritance of a sin nature through Adam's seed, "But each one is tempted when he is drawn away by his own desires and enticed," (James 1:14), you had enough sin on your own that needed to be confessed, so you can't blame Adam for it all.

And I see you asking, "What do you believe?" I'll answer by quoting Paul once again: "For as in Adam all die, even so in Christ all shall be made alive." (1 Corinthians 15:22) And how are we made alive in Christ? Through His blood.

IN THE BLOOD

The Bible is a bloody book. We as truth warriors shouldn't apologize for it, nor try to dumb it down, "for the life of all flesh is its blood." (Leviticus 17:14) And we know that "without shedding of blood there is no remission." (Hebrews 9:22)

> "Then Jesus said to them, 'Most assuredly, I say to you, unless you eat the flesh of the Son of Man and drink His blood, you have no life in you. Whoever eats My flesh and drinks My blood has eternal life, and I will raise him up at the last day. For My flesh is food indeed, and My blood is drink indeed. He who eats My flesh and drinks My blood abides in Me, and I in him.'"
>
> (John 6:53-56)

The New Testament, according to the words of Jesus, is His blood shed for many for the remission of sins. (Matthew 26:28)

This blood of Jesus' is so precious, so costly, so perfect, there is nothing on this earth to compare with its exquisiteness. It is innocent blood shed by the God-Man for your sins, my sins, his sins, her sins, their sins, our sins. It cleanses all sin. (1 John 1:7)

Imagine what Moses would have thought, way back then, had he known his participation in the sacrifices of the Israelites (Exodus 24:8) was a foreshadowing of the culmination of very God Himself as the Man Jesus Christ offering His own blood for those who believed in Him? What a heritage we have received! There is no other religion that comes close to the majesty and simplistic beauty of the shed blood of Jesus Christ. That in and of itself, apart from any other experience I've had, proves to me it is the "right" religion.

That is why it is also the most reviled of all religions. Indeed, Zipporah was right in calling Moses a "bloody husband." (Exodus 4:26)

It is our right, privilege and duty, through our position in Christ, through His blood, that we as truth warriors are able to operate in a supernatural way to show that Jesus' blood destroys the works of iniquity and sin. Life, truly, is in the blood.

> "Now may the God of peace who brought up our Lord Jesus from the dead, that great Shepherd of the sheep, through the blood of the everlasting covenant, make you complete in every good work to do His will, working in you what is well pleasing in His sight, through Jesus Christ, to whom be glory forever and ever. Amen."
>
> (Hebrews 13:20-21)

III THE TRUTH OF III
THE HOLY SPIRIT

The third and final Person of the Godhead is the Holy Spirit. Of course, speaking of preeminence and deity, the designation of "third and final" does not mean in a sense of order or position. By now you know this. However, as the ministry of the Spirit to the body of Christ is the age we live in now, and directly relates to an expression of the supernatural in the lives of truth warriors, we are studying Him last.

The theology of the Holy Spirit is fairly simple to understand: He, like the Father and Son, is coequally and eternally God, worthy of worship and adoration. The substance of His existence is identical and the same as that of Jesus and the Creator, and while He can be distinguished in expression from the Son and the Father, He cannot be separated from Them as a detached deity. He is elementally the one God. Just as the expression of Jesus points to the Father, the expression of the Holy Spirit points to

Jesus, so thus, both pointing to the expression of the Father, who in turn points to Them, in perfect trinity of existence.

The Spirit of God is omnipresent, omniscient, omnipotent. He is eternal, with no end, no beginning. Just like the Father and the Son, He is, indeed, called God in the Bible (1 Corinthians 12:4-6, as just one reference of many.) He is the Spirit of life, which means life originates in Him, just as in the Father and the Son. (Romans 8:2) Without His operation, life would not have existed, the same as with the Father and the Son.

He was present at creation and a vital part of it, actually hovering over the waters (Genesis 1:2) and is present throughout the entire Word of God to Revelation (22:17.) When God breathed into man's nostrils, he became a living being (Genesis 2:7), the same as when Jesus breathed upon His disciples and told them, "Receive the Holy Spirit," signifying the new birth. (John 20:22) The Spirit is the breath of God that quickens life.

Man was made to be the temple of the Holy Spirit, the physical housing of a spiritual Being. When God created man in His image, his relationship was with the entire Trinity, the Creator, the Word (Logos) of God (Jesus) and the Spirit of God. When man fell into sin, the communication was broken between the Creator and the created—the fellowship with the Father, the Holy Spirit and the Word was lost as part of the penal consequences of sin.

"And the Lord said, 'My Spirit shall not strive with man forever, for he is indeed flesh...'" (Genesis 6:3) The Septuagint, Syriac, Targum and Vulgate translations use the word "abide" for "strive."

When man fell, the Spirit withdrew from the human heart, because He is HOLY. When He left, man died—spiritually and ultimately physically. Man's nature became corrupted. (John 3:6)

This does not imply that the Holy Spirit had *nothing* to do with man, any more than the preincarnate Son or Father completely abandoned interaction with the fallen creation. The Lord made a covenant with Abraham, and because of Abraham's faith in that covenant, it was accounted to him for righteousness (right-standing) with God—just as today, when we place faith in the New Covenant offered through Jesus, we are considered righteous before the Lord. The promised Seed of Abraham, in the fullness of time, has also permitted us, the Gentiles, to be justified by faith in that same Seed, and we have received the promised Spirit in all the amplitude of His gifts and grace. (See Genesis 18:1-15, 22:18; Galatians 3; Romans 4.)

And even though the Spirit was imparted sparingly in the Old Testament, shrouded and veiled in the elements of the Law before the mind of men, even the Mosaic era shows that He was not entirely absent from man, according to Numbers 21:7, 27:18 and Deuteronomy 34:9. Further, the times of the Judges and Prophets of the OT show the external influence of the Holy Spirit coming upon mankind; however, due to the corruption of man's nature, the Spirit did not reside *in* man. Rather, He came upon man from the outside and would "lift off"—as in the cases of Samson and Saul. (Judges 14:6; 16:20; 1 Samuel 16:14)

The plan of restoring complete communication with the Creator involved the Word being made flesh, to be a Mediator between the Father and fallen man. But also once the second Adam fulfilled the requirements of the Law by bearing sin in His own body and paying the punishment by His death, the Holy Spirit could then return into man with grace and power that would be forfeited never again. (See 1 Peter 3:18-20; 1:11.)

Just as He is the Spirit of life, the very breath of God, He not only restored life to Christ's body (Romans 8:11) but restored life to man spiritually and physically by inhabiting redeemed mankind once again. The Holy Spirit actually lives inside you as a born-again person.

It is, therefore, fallacy and dangerously ignorant to proclaim the Holy Spirit is merely a force or energy, a power that does not have a distinct persona. We as truth warriors would *lose* that personal relationship with one third of the Godhead's expression. Imagine the dire consequences!

Just as God the Father is a Spirit, the Spirit is a Spirit. (Clever.) That means even though neither have a corporeal body, it does not make Them any less distinctly a divine Person. Even though the Spirit is referred to as Wind or Breath, this does not imply He is simply a *thing*. It is insulting and irreverent to say so.

The Greek word for "spirit" is *pneuma*, as in pneumatic or pneumonia. This is Strong's (#4151, something like "PYOO-mah") partial definition of *pneuma*:

1. the third person of the triune God, the Holy Spirit, coequal, coeternal with the Father and the Son
   a. sometimes referred to in a way which emphasises his personality and character (the \Holy\ Spirit)
   b. sometimes referred to in a way which emphasises his work and power (the Spirit of \Truth\)
   c. never referred to as a depersonalised force
2. a movement of air (a gentle blast)
   a. of the wind, hence the wind itself
   b. breath of nostrils or mouth

The Holy Spirit is unseen, just like wind or breath—but His effects can be felt the same as the earthly correlations. Further, to call Him "it" is to cheapen His existence. In His earthly teachings, Jesus referred to the Spirit consistently using personal pronouns, and in the masculine gender (technically the word *pneuma* is gender neutral.) For one scriptural reference of many, I refer you to John 14:15-17.

The Spirit has emotions. He can be insulted and angered, grieved, shocked and abused (blasphemy.) He is a teacher, an instructor; He reproves; He testifies; He searches all things; and He even prays! Like you, He has a mind and makes decisions.

You want the Scriptures, huh? Good students! Here are a few: 2 Samuel 23:2; Isaiah 63:10; Matthew 12:31; John 14:26, 15:26, 16:8; Acts 13:2; Romans 8:26-27; Ephesians 4:30; 1 Corinthians 2:10, 12:11. And just bunches of others—but these ones jumped out at me.

The point is it is our great privilege, unspeakable joy, to have a divine Person indwelling our bodies as born-again believers. I love the Holy Spirit; don't you?

Jesus referred to the Spirit in His command to baptize believers in the names of all three of the Trinity. Therefore, the Spirit is on equal ground with the Son and the Father. If you believe Jesus is God, if you believe the Father is God, you must believe the Spirit is God. Jesus portrayed Himself, the Father and the Spirit as being one. (John 16) Ephesians 2:18 shows us that through Jesus, by the Spirit, we have access to the Father.

So, if we accept the established truth of the Spirit as a Person, let's identify how this Person operates.

THE WORK OF THE SPIRIT

Prior to the Ascension of Jesus, the Spirit's work was a little different than today—or rather, how He operated was different. Genesis 1 shows that He was active in the Creation, and He is active still in the preservation of that Creation. He has just as much role in sustaining the universe as God the Father and God the Son. No life could happen apart from the Spirit's existence, any more than it could apart from the Father or Jesus. The Spirit helped take the earth when it was formless and void and shape it into the reality we know today. After the Fall, we highlighted briefly the Spirit's work concerning mankind, from an external perspective, coming upon them and then lifting off, for it took the regeneration of the new birth before the Spirit could once again inhabit mankind.

Now, in the Church Age, specifically after Christ ascended and the Spirit was released on Pentecost in Acts 2, through to this very hour, the Spirit's primary activity concerns working with the saints, from the inside to the outside, in cultivating godly, holy living. He is our great Comforter, and there is a passive side to this comfort He provides, in a friendly, mothering sense; and there is an aggressive side where the Spirit works passionately to ensure we make good the provisions of the cross.

Since this book is intended to be an introductory discourse on the glory of the Godhead, and how it pertains to our lives as truth warriors—I will save the more in-depth teaching on the help of the Holy Spirit for *Overwhelmed by the Spirit*.

But for the purposes of this book, we need to look at another facet of the Spirit's work: that is, to convict the world of sin, righteousness and judgment.

> "And when He has come, He will convict the world of sin, and of righteousness, and of judgment: of sin, because they do not believe in Me; of righteousness, because I go to My Father and you see Me no more; of judgment, because the ruler of this world is judged."
>
> (John 16:8-11)

The concept of conviction, such as we mean it in this book, is such that evidence is so well presented, the person comes to an understanding of their own guilt. They see for themselves that they are wrong. In other words what condemns them is their own sin; the Holy Spirit just brings it to their understanding. They acknowledge it; He points it out. This is why they were "cut to the heart" in Acts 2.

And while it is true that once we become born again, we are no longer condemned by our previous sins, I have seen a recent, alarming move in the Body that says the Holy Spirit no longer convicts us when we err. (The premise being either a) we can no longer sin or b) all sins, past, present and future, are already forgiven, so there is no point in conviction.)

Of course, it is a fine line we must walk, not wavering to either extreme side of the street, because I do not believe the Holy Spirit brings condemnation (unconfessed, habitual sin can do that in and of itself)—but I also believe that we are still in need of a lifestyle of repentance to see the greatest work of the Spirit in our daily walks.

That is not to say we live under condemnation, nor constant conviction of guilt, but rather that we do not become callous toward sin.

A conviction also simply means to be fervently "convinced" of something: i.e., I am convinced in my convictions that sin is death and the Spirit is life; therefore choose life.

I see a lot of confusion in many circles surrounding the above excerpt from John 16. Really, I don't think it's a very difficult concept, especially when we look at "convicts" as "convinces." The Spirit's work is to convince the world of sin, righteousness and judgment, all for the reasons the Lord gave: sin, because they don't believe in Christ; righteousness, because Christ returned to the Father and His blood made men righteous (who believe on Him); and judgment because the devil is judged according to sin, and the effects of sin in our lives are overturned.

Really, the righteousness of Christ is what the Holy Spirit specifically shows the world. We are only made righteous in the eyes of God because of *His* righteousness. His own righteousness so far surpasses ours as to be qualified as "far above all principality and power and might and dominion, and every name that is named, **not only in this age but also in that which is to come.**" (Ephesians 1:21, **emphasis added**)

Therefore, the judgment the Holy Spirit convinces the world of is not of Christ, but rather of the devil. Indeed, Satan was judged when Christ was crucified and rose from the grave.

Some of us tend to downplay this truth of judgment, but you and I as truth warriors have been convinced by the Spirit of the certainty that the enemy has been judged, and that there will be future judgment into eternity for those who reject Christ.

Judgment is one of the most overlooked aspects of eschatology in my opinion. I am not speaking of critical fault-finding but righteous judgment (and its sister counterpart, discernment): rightly dividing the black-and-white of what is error and death, and what is right and life; our provisions purchased at the cross, and the future consequences of spurning those provisions.

We as truth warriors are called to judge rightly, to decide as the Spirit would decide. (See 1 Corinthians 6.)

Another facet of the Spirit's work is to anoint us as truth warriors with a supernatural unction both in our personal lives and in our expressions of ministry to others. This is the *personal* anointing that produces godly living (the fruit of the Spirit) and the *ministerial* anointing that produces godly acts (the gifts of the Spirit) in the lives of others as a means of bringing them into their own personal anointing.

Jesus was anointed by the Spirit (Luke 4:18; Acts 10:38), and it was by this anointing that He did what He did in the name of miraculous ministry as a Man.

We, following Christ's example, must cultivate an honor and, indeed, a desire for the anointing—that is, to *thicken* it, as in the holy anointing oil is thickened—we must have a yearning for it (the anointing for the fruit, the anointing for the gifts) and covet its presence. This is not wrong, because what we are in actuality coveting is the Spirit Himself, who *is* the singular Gift of 1 Corinthians 12 and who *is* the singular Fruit of Galatians 5, in all of His manifestations and expressions. We are simply coveting more of Him! As we honor His presence in our lives, He in turn entrusts to us the manifestations of His reputation to the people at large.

I have gone to great lengths to outline the anointing of the Holy Spirit, so I will refer you to my other books for a greater explanation—but as far as truth goes, and our warring for it, the work of the Spirit in anointing us cannot be underplayed or talked away.

Just as the Spirit testifies of Christ (John 15:26-27), I believe the Spirit also bears witness of us, as we yield to Him as Teacher and Lord, showing forth fruit and gifts that call to the lost, uplift the brethren, and indeed, turn us into truth warriors of the supernatural!

☷ ABOUT THE ☷ AUTHOR

JAMES MALONEY has been in full-time ministry for nearly forty years as the president of The ACTS Group International. As a well-respected prophetic voice, James' ministry expression is marked by a powerful sign-and-wonder flow, heavily geared toward healing for the mind, soul and body.

But James' life began with abuse, rejection and fear. As a teenager, facing suicidal thoughts, he cried out for an answer: "God, if You're really real, You're going to have to reveal Yourself to me, because I can't take this anymore!"

Jesus Christ provided that answer, appearing in a cloud of glory with two outstretched hands: "I have heard your cry for acceptance. I have heard your cry for reality, and I love you just the way that you are."

Since that life-altering encounter, the Lord's anointing and grace has manifested through James' ministry in a prophetic seer operation, where specific details about people's conditions are supernaturally revealed, thereby creating faith in Jesus Christ to receive their miracle. To God's honor alone, this panoramic flow has been consistently used to dissolve metal in people's bodies, to create or recreate limbs, to liquefy tumors and pacemakers, to open blind eyes and deaf ears, and much more!

As an accomplished theologian, James holds a D.D., a Th.D., and a Ph.D. He taught in Bible schools for over twenty years and has authored several exciting books: *The Dancing Hand of God*, *The Panoramic Seer*, *Overwhelmed by the Spirit* and *The Wounded Cry*. He is also the compiler of *Ladies of Gold* and *Rapture in the Middle East*, the collected teachings of Frances Metcalfe and the Golden Candlestick.

James and his wife, Joy, live in the Dallas-Fort Worth area with their grown children and six grandsons. He can be reached via the ministry's website at www.answeringthecry.com.